JOHN GREGORY-SMITH

THE GREATEST TRAYBAKE COOKBOOK <u>EVER</u>

PENGUIN MICHAEL JOSEPH

UK | USA | Canada | Ireland | Australia
India | New Zealand | South Africa

Penguin Michael Joseph is part of the Penguin Random House group of companies whose addresses can be found at global.penguinrandomhouse.com

Penguin Random House UK, One Embassy Gardens, 8 Viaduct Gardens, London SW11 7BW

penguin.co.uk

First published 2026
004

Text copyright © John Gregory-Smith, 2026
Photography copyright © Martin Poole, 2026

The moral right of the author has been asserted

Penguin Random House values and supports copyright. Copyright fuels creativity, encourages diverse voices, promotes freedom of expression and supports a vibrant culture. Thank you for purchasing an authorized edition of this book and for respecting intellectual property laws by not reproducing, scanning or distributing any part of it by any means without permission. You are supporting authors and enabling Penguin Random House to continue to publish books for everyone. No part of this book may be used or reproduced in any manner for the purpose of training artificial intelligence technologies or systems.

In accordance with Article 4(3) of the DSM Directive 2019/790, Penguin Random House expressly reserves this work from the text and data mining exception

Set in Boston Skyline Sans Clean, Prequel, Oriet, BlueCreek, and DIN Pro

Colour reproduction by Altaimage Ltd
Printed and bound in Great Britain by Bell and Bain Ltd, Glasgow

The authorized representative in the EEA is Penguin Random House Ireland, Morrison Chambers, 32 Nassau Street, Dublin, D02 YH68

A CIP catalogue record for this book is available from the British Library

ISBN: 978-0-241-74641-7

Penguin Random House is committed to a sustainable future for our business, our readers and our planet. This book is made from Forest Stewardship Council® certified paper.

THE GREATEST TRAYBAKE COOKBOOK EVER

JOHN GREGORY-SMITH

PHOTOGRAPHY BY MARTIN POOLE

CONTENTS

INTRODUCTION — 6
ABOUT THIS BOOK — 10
WHAT YOU'LL NEED — 12

CHAPTER 1.
SPEEDY RECIPES — 14

CHAPTER 2.
CHICKEN RECIPES — 56

CHAPTER 3.
SWANKY RECIPES — 100

CHAPTER 4.
SLOW RECIPES — 130

CHAPTER 5.
RICE AND PASTA RECIPES — 164

CHAPTER 6.
SIDES AND DIPS RECIPES — 198

INDEX — 226
THANKS — 232

INTRODUCTION

The excitement I feel about this book is beyond words. At last I get to say it: Welcome to *The Greatest Traybake Cookbook Ever*! Wow, that sounds good. For the longest time I was 'that guy' known for writing elegant Eastern Mediterranean coffee-table cookbooks. Don't get me wrong, I loved doing them, but I simply didn't have permission to write something like this. Thanks to social media, everything changed. Building an amazing online community has allowed me to step beyond my Middle Eastern culinary roots and dive into an arena of quick and easy recipes inspired by cuisines I adore from all around the world. These recipes seem to have struck a chord – my social media following grows daily and I cook for millions of people on a morning TV show that I just adore.

I'll always have a soft spot for Middle Eastern food and the way every dish feels like a celebration, with vibrant garnishes and beautiful perfumed aromas. Plus I am a kebab and hummus fan for life. But as someone who has travelled extensively, what excites me just as much is discovering what people are eating in other places. Whether it's a street-food cart in a dusty village, a cosy family dinner in the mountains or finding a hole-in-the-wall in a new city, there is much deliciousness everywhere. Swanky restaurant dishes I am less fussed about. They're lovely and all, but it's not my vibe for everyday cooking. I'm happy to leave the foam and fiddle to someone else.

What I love most is taking inspiration from my travels, and lately from random YouTube videos of village life in Middle Eastern countries. I like to borrow elements from classic dishes or throw in an unexpected ingredient to make something new that still feels easy and familiar. I do stick to the hard-and-fast rule of keeping the recipes supermarket-friendly. Nothing kills your cooking buzz faster than realizing you can't get half the ingredients you need without a delivery from a specialist store in a different country that happens to be shut anyway.

Here's something I learned early on: if you want people to try something new, keep it simple. That's why traybakes are the ultimate entry point. Every time I share traybake recipes on social media, they pop off. I can't tell you what a joy it is when someone I've never met cooks one of my recipes. Knowing they took a punt on me to try something new is such a privilege.

Social media has been a whirlwind. It began with a full-on COVID pivot when everything else fell apart. I started filming recipes at home, roping in my mum or my nieces and nephews to be my makeshift crew. They all breathed a sigh of relief when I discovered what a tripod was. I honestly have no idea how it took off, but with a lot of hard work it did. Fast forward a couple of years and I've got over a million Instagram followers, half a million on TikTok and a solid following on YouTube and Threads. I share what I love: food that's so good you'll want to 'face-plant' into it (as I often say). If it's truly yummy, it makes the cut.

Traybakes have become a solid staple on my channels. I've loved playing around with them, using unexpected ingredients that you wouldn't typically associate with traybakes and things like uncooked pasta and rice. My mum and dad will confirm I've always done the opposite of what anyone tells me, sometimes to my credit and other times (like refusing to cut my Sun-In orange hair in the 90s) not so much, but I feel those stories are for another time!

The recipes in this book really are some of the most creative cooking I have ever done. I am over the moon to share them with you, and I hope you love them all as much as I do. As a budding social media mogul, nothing makes me happier than seeing your creations, so don't forget to tag me in your supper snaps or slide into my DMs with questions. You'll find me at @johngs on all platforms. I'll see you there.

Cheers,

John G-S x

ABOUT THIS BOOK

When I started thinking about a traybake cookbook and trying to come up with one hundred recipes that would be so lip-smackingly good they would become weekly staples, I had to lean into what really works in a traybake and what doesn't. Some ingredients and techniques simply don't work (like certain cuts of meat that need a proper sear in a hot pan, not the gentle tickle of an oven), so I avoided those and focused on what truly shines. Every recipe in this book has been fine-tuned to make the most of your roasting tin. Sometimes that means layering in ingredients at different times or adjusting the cooking temperature, but my goal is always to keep things as quick and easy as possible. Many of these recipes are true 'one-tray wonders': chuck everything into the tin, hurl it in the oven and you're done.

Every recipe in this book is easy enough to throw together in the week and lush enough to serve on the weekend. I cover quick and easy dinners as well as swanky suppers for when you want to pull out all the stops. There's a whole chapter dedicated to chicken (my dad would kill me if that wasn't here), rice and pasta for my carb lovers, and some of my favourite sides and dips because who doesn't love a dip? There's a section on slow cooking because traybakes are a great way to transform raggedy old cuts of meat into the belle of the ball. There are comfort food classics, al fresco feasts and easy family meals – it's all here.

(V) = Vegetarian

WHAT YOU'LL NEED

Now, let's talk gear. The oven is your best friend for traybakes, but there are a few things to keep in mind. First, always preheat your oven. My mum's 'turn it on 30 seconds before you need it and hope for the best' method doesn't quite cut it. Give your oven a good 10 to 15 minutes to heat up (all ovens have a nifty little light that tells you exactly when they have reached the right temperature). And invest in some decent oven gloves! Mine are very loud neon green ones that I stole from my gorgeous fiancé, Srdan. There're not lookers but they are indestructible, and I can hold a hot roasting tin forever without burning myself. Function over fashion always at the oven (and never anywhere else!).

Speaking of roasting tins, I've kept it simple for this book. I've used only two sizes: a large 30x40cm non-stick tin that's perfect when you need space to char and a smaller 24x32cm aluminium baking tin, ideal when you want to keep things saucy. Size really does matter when it comes to a good roasting, but I didn't want each recipe to require a different tin, because who has time for that? I reference where to use baking paper and foil to lock in moisture and when to line a roasting tin if you don't have a non-stick tray. I hope this keeps each recipe really easy to make so you can use this book over and over again.

CUMIN-SPICED LAMB CHOPS WITH ROASTED SQUASH	16
SMOKY PORK MEATBALL PAPRIKASH	18
QUICK-FIRE CHIMICHURRI SALMON	20
CREAMY HARISSA SAUSAGE CASSEROLE	22
BROCCOLI, GOAT'S CHEESE AND ZA'ATAR FRITTATA	24
HARISSA BEEF MEATBALLS AND GIANT COUSCOUS	26
PARMA-WRAPPED COD WITH SMOKY CHICKPEA STEW	28
CRISPY CAULIFLOWER SALAD WITH JALAPEÑO AND SOURED CREAM DRESSING	30
SPEEDY PRAWN SAGANAKI	32
LAMB KOFTA WITH CHIPS AND DIPS	34
HARISSA SALMON WITH CRISPY LENTILS AND GARLICKY YOGHURT	36
CRISPY FIRECRACKER TOFU	38
VIETNAMESE-STYLE CHARRED HISPI CABBAGE	40
STICKY MUSHROOM BAO BUNS	42
ISTANBUL EXPRESS BEEF STEW	44
CREAMY TAHINI CHICKPEA STEW	46
NEXT-LEVEL CHORIZO SHAKSHUKA	48
MOROCCAN-STYLE CREAMY COCONUT LENTIL SOUP	50
COCONUT, CORIANDER AND LIME COD	52
MELTED LEEKS WITH GARLICKY YOGHURT AND CHILLI BUTTER	54

SPEEDY RECIPES

This is the ultimate collection of quick and easy traybakes, perfect for those moments when hunger strikes, but time is not on your side. These recipes keep things simple, using minimal ingredients and requiring little prep, while delivering delicious results in 35 minutes' cooking time or less. Whether you're grabbing a bite before dashing out the door, unwinding on the sofa after a long day, hosting friends for dinner, or feeding a hungry family, there's something here to make your life easier and tastier.

CUMIN-SPICED LAMB CHOPS
WITH ROASTED SQUASH

1 squash, cut into 0.5–1cm cubes (about 550g in total)

4 tbsp olive oil

1 x 400g tin of chickpeas, drained and rinsed

300g cherry tomatoes, halved

2½ tsp garam masala

4 cloves of garlic, peeled and crushed

½ tsp ground cumin

¼ tsp ground fenugreek

8 lamb chops (about 700g in total)

300g Greek yoghurt – I use 10% fat

2 tbsp lime pickle

a handful of roughly chopped coriander leaves

salt and pepper

When you're short on time but want something that feels a little fancy, this Indian-style traybake is a lifesaver. Tiny cubes of butternut squash – small enough to roast quickly – go golden and crispy in the oven with some hearty chickpeas. Spiced lamb chops and cherry tomatoes are layered on top, and their juices marry together to create a lovely mellow sauce. To finish, I love a generous dollop of lime pickle yoghurt that melts so satisfyingly over everything on your plate.

SERVES 4

1
Preheat the oven to 220°C/200°C fan/gas 7. Chuck the squash into a 30x40cm roasting tin and add 1 tablespoon of the olive oil and a good pinch of salt and pepper. Toss together and roast for 10 minutes to start softening the squash.

2
Put the chickpeas, cherry tomatoes, 1 tablespoon of olive oil, 1 teaspoon of garam masala and a good pinch of salt and pepper into a mixing bowl and toss together. Add to the tray with the squash. Mix well and return to the oven for 10 minutes.

3
Meanwhile, put the remaining 2 tablespoons of oil into a large mixing bowl. Add the garlic, the remaining 1½ teaspoons of garam masala, the cumin, fenugreek and a good pinch of salt and pepper. Mix well, then chuck in the lamb chops and mix together.

4
Arrange the chops on top of the squash in the roasting tin and roast in the oven for 8 to 10 minutes or until the lamb is cooked on the outside but still pink in the middle.

5
While the lamb cooks, mix the yoghurt with the lime pickle and a good pinch of salt and pepper.

6
Scatter the coriander over the lamb, chickpeas and veg and divide between four serving plates. Serve immediately with big dollops of yoghurt on the side.

PREP:
15 minutes

COOK:
30 minutes

SMOKY PORK MEATBALL PAPRIKASH

2 onions, peeled and finely sliced
2 tbsp olive oil
500g minced pork – I use 20% fat
2 tsp garlic powder
3 tsp paprika, plus extra to serve
300ml hot chicken stock – from 1 stock cube
3 tbsp tomato puree
100g soured cream
a few finely chopped chives
salt and pepper

Paprikash is a classic Hungarian stew bursting with vibrant paprika – a dish you might not have heard of until now. My version features juicy pork meatballs gently simmered in a lush creamy tomato and paprika sauce. It's incredibly simple to make and so comforting. It's one of my favourite TV dinners. You'll notice there's no carb in the recipe, but before you hurl the book across the room, that was intentional, because you could go in several directions here. Think buttery pasta, creamy mashed potatoes or fragrant rice. You pick the vibe and go for it.

SERVES 4

1
Preheat the oven to 220°C/200°C fan/gas 7. Pop the onions into a 24x32cm roasting tin. Add the olive oil and season with salt and pepper. Toss together and roast for 18 to 20 minutes or until they are looking soft and charred.

2
Meanwhile, mix the pork together with 1 teaspoon of the garlic powder, 1 teaspoon of the paprika and a good pinch of salt and pepper. Roll into 16 little meatballs.

3
Whisk together the chicken stock, tomato puree, the remaining 1 teaspoon garlic powder, the remaining 2 teaspoons of paprika and a good pinch of salt and pepper.

4
Reduce the oven temperature to 200°C/180°C fan/gas 6, remove the tin and give the onions a good mix. Pour in the stock. Add the meatballs and return to the oven for 10 to 15 minutes until the meatballs are just cooked through.

5
Stir the soured cream into the sauce and check the seasoning, adding salt and pepper to taste. Garnish with the chives and a big pinch of paprika. Serve immediately.

PREP:
15 minutes

COOK:
35 minutes

QUICK-FIRE CHIMICHURRI SALMON

for the salmon:

250g tenderstem broccoli, trimmed and any thick stems cut in half lengthways

250g asparagus, trimmed

150g cherry tomatoes

2 tbsp olive oil

4 salmon fillets (500–600g in total)

salt and pepper

for the chimichurri:

a large handful of parsley leaves

a large handful of coriander leaves

2 spring onions, roughly chopped

1 red chilli, deseeded if you like

1 clove of garlic, peeled

6 tbsp olive oil

3 tbsp red wine vinegar

1 tsp dried oregano

Traybakes are a vibe all year round, and in the summer this is what you want to be eating, especially if you're short on time. A lovely light salmon traybake, gently cooked until just tender with plenty of crunchy vegetables and a zingy chimichurri sauce. This Argentine-inspired dressing is to die for. It's packed with fragrant herbs, a little kick of chilli and a splash of vinegar that gives it such a moreish tang.

SERVES 4

1
Preheat the oven to 220°C/200°C fan/gas 7. Pop the broccoli, asparagus and cherry tomatoes into a 30x40cm roasting tin. Add the oil and a good pinch of salt and pepper. Toss together and roast in the oven for 10 minutes to start softening the veg.

2
Meanwhile, make the chimichurri. Chuck the parsley, coriander, spring onions, chilli and the garlic clove into a food processor or mini chopper. Blitz until fine, then add the olive oil, vinegar, dried oregano and plenty of salt and pepper. Blitz until smooth.

3
Place the salmon fillets skin side down on a plate and pat dry with some kitchen paper. Season with a little salt, then spoon half a tablespoon of the chimichurri over each fillet, spreading it out evenly. Set the salmon to one side while the veg cooks.

4
Put the salmon, chimichurri side up, into the roasting tin amongst the vegetables and roast for 8 to 10 minutes or until the salmon is just cooked through. Serve immediately with the remaining chimichurri at the table.

PREP:
10 minutes

COOK:
20 minutes

CREAMY HARISSA SAUSAGE CASSEROLE

8 pork sausages (about 500g in total)
1 onion, peeled and finely chopped
1 tbsp olive oil
2 x 400g tins of butter beans
1 x 400g tin of chopped tomatoes
100g pitted Kalamata olives
2 cloves of garlic, peeled and crushed
1 tbsp rose harissa
1 tsp ras el hanout
optional: 50ml double cream
salt and pepper

This speedy traybake is a delightful fusion of flavours, blending British classics with Moroccan flair. British bangers, one of the most versatile quick-cook ingredients out there, are cooked in a warming Moroccan-inspired butter-bean stew flavoured with ras el hanout spice mix and rose harissa. Now, if you've been following me for a while, you'll know I have a medium-to-mega obsession with rose harissa. It literally makes anything taste delicious. One tablespoon gives a nice hum to this dish, but if you're craving a kick, try adding an extra tablespoon into the sauce. The cream is an optional extra for when you feel like you need a little more comfort in your life. It's equally lush without, so I'll leave that bit up to you. It's your call!

SERVES 4

1
Preheat the oven to 240°C/220°C fan/gas 9. Pop the sausages, onion, olive oil and a pinch of salt and pepper into a 24x32cm roasting tin. Mix well and put into the oven to roast for 15 minutes to get some colour on to everything.

2
Remove the roasting tin from the oven and reduce the temperature to 220°C/200°C fan/gas 7. Drain one tin of butter beans and add them to the roasting tin. Add the other tin of beans with all its liquid and the tomatoes, olives, garlic, rose harissa, ras el hanout and a good pinch of salt and pepper. Mix well and return to the oven for 20 minutes until everything is bubbling. Add the double cream, if using, stir together and serve immediately.

PREP:
5 minutes

COOK:
35 minutes

BROCCOLI, GOAT'S CHEESE
AND ZA'ATAR FRITTATA

10 medium free-range eggs
100ml double cream
150g extra mature Cheddar cheese, grated
1 tbsp za'atar, plus extra to serve
250g tenderstem broccoli
2 tbsp olive oil
150g goat's cheese, thinly sliced
½ a red onion, peeled and finely sliced
juice of ½ a lemon
2 large handfuls of mint leaves
salt and pepper

On those sunny days when you're in the mood for something light, tasty and effortless, this frittata is an absolute game-changer. It's infused with a generous pinch of mighty za'atar – a vibrant Lebanese spice blend that really packs a punch – and creamy goat's cheese, then topped with a zingy onion salad. Now, if you have any leftovers, you're in for a treat. They make the perfect lunch 'al desko' in the office the next day.

SERVES 4

1
Line a 24x32cm roasting tin with baking paper and pop it into the oven. Preheat the oven to 200ºC/180ºC fan/gas 6 and let the roasting tin heat up.

2
Crack the eggs into a bowl. Add the double cream, Cheddar, za'atar and a big pinch of salt and pepper. Whisk together.

3
Trim the broccoli and cut most of the stems in half lengthways so they cook quickly. Put into a mixing bowl and add 1 tablespoon of the oil and a pinch of salt and pepper. Toss together.

4
Carefully pour the egg mixture into the hot roasting tin and give it a stir to even out the cheese. Arrange the slices of goat's cheese and the broccoli over the top. Return to the oven for 12 to 15 minutes or until the eggs are just set in the middle and the goat's cheese all oozy.

5
Meanwhile, chuck the red onion into a mixing bowl and add the lemon juice and a pinch of salt. Toss together and leave for 5 minutes to soften a little. Add the mint and the last 1 tablespoon of olive oil and toss together just before serving.

6
Arrange the salad over the cooked frittata and serve immediately with extra za'atar for sprinkling.

PREP:
10 minutes

COOK:
15 minutes

HARISSA BEEF MEATBALLS
AND GIANT COUSCOUS

300g giant (or pearl) couscous
1½ tsp baharat
700ml hot chicken stock – from 1 stock cube
500g minced beef – I use 15–20% fat
2 tbsp rose harissa, plus extra to serve
2 cloves of garlic, peeled and crushed
300g Greek yoghurt – I use 10% fat
a handful of finely chopped parsley leaves
80g watercress
juice of ½ a lemon
1 tbsp olive oil
salt and pepper

Cooking juicy harissa meatballs over a bed of giant couscous in the oven is so deeply satisfying. As the meatballs roast, their juices seep into the couscous, making it wonderfully soft and flavourful. Now, these are quick-cook meatballs. No egg or breadcrumbs here. I use rose harissa for flavour and a dollop of yoghurt to help bind them. Chuck in a simple watercress salad and a little more yoghurt and you have an effortless yet elegant speedy supper.

SERVES 4

1
Preheat the oven to 200°C/180°C fan/gas 6. Chuck the couscous, baharat, stock and a good pinch of salt and pepper into a 24x32cm roasting tin. Stir together and roast for 10 minutes to soften the couscous.

2
Meanwhile, put the beef into a mixing bowl and add the rose harissa, garlic, 2 tablespoons of the yoghurt and a good pinch of salt and pepper. Mix well and roll into 12 meatballs.

3
Place the meatballs on top of the couscous. Pour in 80ml of water and return to the oven for 12 to 15 minutes or until the meatballs are just cooked through but still very juicy. Rain down the parsley just before serving.

4
Meanwhile, chuck the watercress into a bowl and add the lemon juice, olive oil and a pinch of salt and pepper. Toss together and serve immediately with the meatballs, the remaining yoghurt and extra rose harissa, if you like.

PREP:
10 minutes

COOK:
25 minutes

PARMA-WRAPPED COD
WITH SMOKY CHICKPEA STEW

2 x 400g tins of chickpeas, drained and rinsed

250g jarred roasted peppers, drained and finely chopped

200g cherry tomatoes, roughly chopped

50g pitted green olives, finely chopped

2 cloves of garlic, peeled and grated

2 tbsp olive oil

100ml white wine

500g tomato passata

2 tsp smoked paprika

a handful of finely chopped parsley leaves

4 cod fillets (about 150g each)

8 slices of Parma ham

salt and pepper

Bursting with bold Spanish flavours, this traybake is a perfect example of how simple store-cupboard staples can create something extraordinary. Olives, chickpeas, tomatoes, smoked paprika and jarred red peppers come together in the oven to form a wonderfully rich stew. This is the base for some beautiful fresh cod fillets that I wrap in cured ham to keep the fish super juicy and really well seasoned in the oven. You can use either Parma or Serrano, whatever you can get your hands on, to deliver that extra savoury kick.

SERVES 4

1
Preheat the oven to 220°C/200°C fan/gas 7. Pat the chickpeas really dry with kitchen paper and chuck them into a 24x32cm roasting tin with the peppers, tomatoes, olives, garlic, olive oil and plenty of salt and pepper. Mix well. Pour in the wine and roast for 10 minutes to get some heat into everything.

2
Add the passata, smoked paprika and most of the parsley to the roasting tin. Season with salt and pepper and stir it all together. Return to the oven for 15 minutes or until the sauce is bubbling.

3
Meanwhile, pat each cod fillet dry, season both sides with salt and pepper and wrap with 2 slices of ham. Place the cod on top of the chickpeas and roast for 8 to 10 minutes or until the ham is a little crispy and the cod just cooked through. Scatter over the remaining parsley and serve immediately.

PREP:
12 minutes

COOK:
35 minutes

CRISPY CAULIFLOWER SALAD
WITH JALAPEÑO AND SOURED CREAM DRESSING

- 1 x 400g tin of chickpeas, drained and rinsed
- 600g cauliflower florets, cut into 2–3cm pieces, plus any little leaves
- 2 tbsp olive oil, plus extra for drizzling
- 1 tsp smoked paprika
- 1 tsp garlic powder
- 1 tsp onion power
- ½ a red onion, peeled and finely chopped
- juice of 1 lemon
- 300g soured cream
- 1 jalapeño, deseeded if you like and finely chopped
- a large handful of finely chopped chives (15g)
- a handful of finely chopped parsley leaves, plus a large handful, roughly chopped, to garnish
- optional: 100g roquefort cheese (or a vegetarian alternative)
- salt

I wouldn't often put the words indulgent and salad together but here we are. This recipe is truly knockout. The cauliflower is doused in spices and roasted until charred and crispy – this is the only way to cook a cauliflower. Boiling or steaming just leaves it lacklustre and gross. There are also chickpeas in there that go gloriously crispy in the oven. I serve this with a jalapeño, chive and soured cream dressing that is lip-smackingly good. And if you are feeling cheeky and love a bit of blue cheese, try crumbling some over the top before you eat. The little nuggets of soft salty cheese make it pop even more.

SERVES 4

1
Preheat the oven to 220ºC/200ºC fan/gas 7. Pat the chickpeas really dry with kitchen paper and chuck them into your 30x40cm roasting tin. Remove any obvious skins, then chuck in the cauliflower, oil, smoked paprika, garlic powder, onion powder and salt. Mix well and drizzle over a little extra oil if you like. Roast for 25 to 30 minutes or until everything is golden and crispy.

2
Meanwhile, put the onion into a bowl with half the lemon juice and a good pinch of salt.

3
Mix the soured cream, jalapeño, chives, parsley, the remaining lemon juice and a good pinch of salt into a gorgeous creamy dressing. You can use a mini chopper to finely chop the chilli and herbs if you want to give the dressing a green colour.

4
To serve, pour the dressing over a serving dish and top with the cauliflower and chickpeas. Scatter over the onions and the roughly chopped parsley leaves. Serve immediately with the blue cheese crumbled over the top, if using.

PREP:
15 minutes

COOK:
30 minutes

SPEEDY PRAWN SAGANAKI

Every summer, I escape to the tiny Greek island of Paxos with my family and it's pure bliss. Think lazy days by the pool with a glass of rosé, heavenly afternoons sailing around secluded coves, and the most incredible food in low-key, unpretentious tavernas. (By the way, you'd probably hate it, so maybe don't bother making the trip.) One of my absolute favourites there is prawn saganaki: juicy prawns in a rich tomato sauce topped with heaps of feta, screaming out for crusty bread to scoop up every last bit. If you've never tried it, here's your sign to tuck in!

SERVES 2

6 spring onions, finely sliced
100g cherry tomatoes, halved
1 clove of garlic, peeled and crushed
½ tsp fennel seeds
1 tbsp + 1 tsp olive oil
500g tomato passata
1 tsp dried oregano
½ tsp chilli flakes
120g feta cheese
180g raw peeled king prawns
a few roughly chopped parsley leaves
salt and pepper

1
Preheat the oven to 200ºC/180ºC fan/gas 6. Chuck the spring onions, cherry tomatoes, garlic, fennel seeds, 1 tablespoon of olive oil and a pinch of salt into a 24x32cm roasting tin. Stir together and pop into the oven for 5 minutes to get the flavours going.

2
Pour the tomato passata into the roasting tin. Add the dried oregano, chilli flakes and plenty of salt and pepper. Break the feta up into big chunks straight into the sauce. Return to the oven for 12 to 15 minutes or until the feta is super soft and charred a little.

3
Mix the prawns with the remaining 1 teaspoon of olive oil and season with salt and pepper. Add them to the roasting tin, poking them into the sauce. Return to the oven for 2 to 3 minutes more or until the prawns are cooked through and coral pink. Serve immediately with a little parsley scattered over the top.

PREP:
8 minutes

COOK:
23 minutes

LAMB KOFTA
WITH CHIPS AND DIPS

1 red onion, peeled and finely sliced into half-moons
1 tbsp + 1 tsp olive oil
400g thin-cut frozen oven chips
500g minced lamb – I use 10% fat
1 tsp baharat
1 tsp dried thyme
zest of 1 lemon
4 cloves of garlic, peeled and crushed
1 tbsp tomato puree
300g yoghurt
200g cherry tomatoes, halved
a small handful of roughly chopped parsley leaves
4 flatbreads
chilli sauce, for drizzling – I use sriracha
salt and pepper

There is something undeniably satisfying about rolling up a rather juicy, fatty kofta in pillowy soft flatbread, with chips that have been cooked with the meat, so they are stodgy and crispy all at the same time. It's a classic way to serve certain kebabs, think Lebanese shawarma or Greek gyros. I love them. Add in a few lush sauces, veggies, pickled chillies if you like them and warm pittas, and you have a fabulous quick and easy feast.

SERVES 4

1
Preheat the oven to 240ºC/220ºC fan/gas 9. Chuck the red onion into a mixing bowl and add 1 teaspoon of the oil and a pinch of salt. Toss together and transfer to a 30x40cm non-stick or lined roasting tin. Add the chips and roast for 5 minutes to get some heat into everything.

2
Meanwhile, put the lamb into a mixing bowl and add the baharat, thyme, half the lemon zest, 3 cloves of crushed garlic, the tomato puree, 2 tablespoons of yoghurt and plenty of salt and pepper. Mix well and divide into eight. Shape each portion into 10cm-long sausage-shaped kofta.

3
Rub the remaining 1 tablespoon of oil over the kofta – I just rub it on to my hands to do this, and then rub the kofta so they get a little oil all over. Put them into the roasting tin, in and around the chips. Add the tomatoes and return to the oven for 12 to 15 minutes or until the lamb is just cooked through and insanely juicy.

4
While that cooks, put the remaining yoghurt into a serving bowl and add the remaining lemon zest and last clove of crushed garlic and stir together.

5
To serve, add a pinch of salt to everything in the roasting tin and scatter over the parsley. Pile up plenty of chips, onions and tomatoes in each flatbread. Top with two of the kofta and loads of yoghurt sauce. Drizzle over as much chilli sauce as you like, wrap up and dive in.

PREP:
15 minutes

COOK:
20 minutes

HARISSA SALMON
WITH CRISPY LENTILS AND GARLICKY YOGHURT

- 2 x 400g tins of beluga lentils, drained and rinsed
- 2 tbsp olive oil, plus extra for drizzling
- 2 tbsp rose harissa paste
- juice of 1 lemon
- 2 tsp runny honey
- 4 x salmon fillets, skin on (500–600g in total)
- 400g Greek yoghurt – I use 10% fat
- 1 clove of garlic, peeled and crushed
- a small handful of finely chopped parsley leaves
- salt

If you need to pluck a swanky dinner out of the air and have very little time to mess around, I've got you covered with this epic salmon traybake. You roast off little beluga lentils with salmon fillets that have been coated in a punchy harissa marinade. The lentils go crispy and the salmon soft and sticky. You serve them up on a slick of garlicky yoghurt, with more harissa marinade drizzled over the top. It's divine.

SERVES 4

1
Preheat the oven to 200ºC/180ºC fan/gas 6. Chuck the lentils into a 30x40cm roasting tin and pat them dry with kitchen paper. Add 1 tablespoon of oil and a good pinch of salt, toss together and roast for 20 minutes until a little crispy at the sides of the tin.

2
Meanwhile, mix the remaining 1 tablespoon of oil with the rose harissa, lemon juice, honey and a good pinch of salt. Spoon half over the salmon fillets, making sure they are completely coated. Leave them to marinate while the lentils cook and set the rest of the harissa dressing aside.

3
Give the pan with the lentils a good shake and push the lentils to the edges of the tray. Put the salmon skin side down into the space you have created in the middle and spoon over any leftover marinade. Pop the tray back into the oven and roast for 10 to 12 minutes or until the salmon is just cooked through.

4
Mix the yoghurt with the garlic and a pinch of salt and swirl on to four serving plates. Top with the crispy lentils and salmon and drizzle over the harissa dressing. Scatter over the parsley and drizzle over a little oil and dive on in.

PREP:
12 minutes

COOK:
32 minutes

CRISPY FIRECRACKER TOFU

This vibrant traybake is an Indian twist on Chinese food, a culture clash of two big cuisines. Alongside a few roasted veggies, it features firm tofu. Now, before you roll your eyes and turn the page, hear me out: tofu is simply a protein-packed vehicle for flavour. Here it crisps up beautifully in the oven, drinking up a bunch of fragrant Indian spices and a sticky, sweet-sour sauce. You can serve it with your choice of rice or noodles. Honestly, it's divine, and I guarantee you'll be going back for more.

SERVES 2

for the tofu:
1 green pepper, cut into 1–2cm pieces
1 red onion, peeled and cut into 1–2cm pieces
2 tbsp groundnut or neutral oil
280g block of extra-firm tofu
2 tbsp cornflour
1 tsp garam masala
¼ tsp hot chilli powder
¼ tsp turmeric
a small handful of finely chopped coriander leaves
salt

for the sauce:
2 tbsp tomato ketchup
2 tbsp white wine vinegar
2 tbsp chilli sauce – I use sriracha
1 tbsp + 1 tsp dark soy sauce
1 tsp caster sugar
2 cloves of garlic, peeled and grated
a 2–3cm piece of fresh ginger, peeled and grated
80ml just-boiled water

PREP:
15 minutes

COOK:
35 minutes

1
Preheat the oven to 220ºC/200ºC fan/gas 7. Put the pepper and onion into a 30x40cm non-stick or lined roasting tin. Add 1 tablespoon of the oil and a little pinch of salt. Toss together and set to one side.

2
Wrap the tofu in a few layers of kitchen paper and squeeze it nice and tight to get out all the excess moisture. Rip 1–2 cm pieces off the block and chuck them into a mixing bowl – this creates lots of uneven surfaces that will go lovely and crispy in the oven.

3
Add the remaining 1 tablespoon of oil to the tofu and a pinch of salt. Toss together to coat, then add the cornflour, garam masala, chilli powder and turmeric. Toss well again and arrange the tofu over the vegetables, spacing out the pieces so they have room to go crispy. Squish any little bits of tofu left in the mixing bowl together to form a new piece and add that as well. Roast in the oven for 30 minutes or until the veg is soft and the tofu crispy.

4
Meanwhile, whisk all the ingredients for the sauce together with a pinch of salt.

5
Remove the roasting tin from the oven. Gently gather the vegetables and tofu into the middle of the roasting tin to help them all get plenty of the sauce over the top. Pour over the sauce and return to the oven for 5 minutes until all bubbly and delicious. Scatter over the coriander and serve immediately.

VIETNAMESE-STYLE CHARRED HISPI CABBAGE

2 hispi cabbages, cut into quarters

2 tbsp groundnut oil

3 tbsp sweet chilli sauce

2 tbsp fish sauce (or vegetarian fish sauce)

juice of 2 limes

2 cloves of garlic, peeled and crushed

2 tsp caster sugar

15g roasted peanuts, crushed

a handful of coriander leaves

½ a red chilli, finely sliced

salt

Let's take a vote: how many of you have ever considered cabbage for dinner? I'm guessing not many hands are raised, but this simple cabbage traybake is an absolute flavour bomb. The star of the show is the beautiful, conical hispi cabbage (also known as sweetheart cabbage), which chars to perfection in the oven. As we all know, roasting is the ultimate way to cook most vegetables, giving us maximum flavour and those ever-so-pleasing crispy edges. Once it's out of the oven, the hot, caramelized cabbage gets doused in a tangy Vietnamese dressing made with fish sauce and lime, which it soaks up wonderfully. Pair it with rice or glass noodles for a more substantial meal. And next time we take a 'cabbage for dinner' vote, I guarantee those hands will shoot straight into the air!

SERVES 4

1
Preheat the oven to 240°C/220°C fan/gas 9. Pop the cabbage, core side up, in a 30x40cm non-stick or lined roasting tray. Drizzle over the oil and season with a pinch of salt. Roast for 15 to 20 minutes until the cabbage is looking lovely and charred but still not quite tender at the stem.

2
Meanwhile, whisk together the sweet chilli sauce, fish sauce, lime juice, garlic and sugar.

3
Remove the cabbage from the oven and reduce the temperature to 200°C/180°C fan/gas 6. Drizzle that dreamy sauce over everything and return to the oven for 4 to 5 minutes or until the cabbage is just tender.

4
To serve, transfer the cabbages to a serving plate. Pour over all the sauce from the roasting tin and garnish with the peanuts, coriander and chilli.

PREP:
5 minutes

COOK:
25 minutes

STICKY MUSHROOM BAO BUNS

My sticky soy-roasted mushroom bao buns are such a lovely quick and easy dinner, and I don't know about you, but I find any build-your-own-meal situation utterly thrilling. It's a hangover from the nineties, when Tex-Mex meal kits swept the nation and you could feast on stuffed taco shells, just like your favourite character from a shiny American movie. Food was very boring back then. This traybake is inspired by Taiwanese *gua bao*, soft pork-filled steamed buns with pickled sour mustard leaves – a good Asian grocery store will have them, but I use sauerkraut as a more accessible alternative – coriander and peanuts. Put everything on the table so you can dive in and make your own.

SERVES 4

750g portobello mushrooms, finely sliced

2 tbsp groundnut or neutral oil

1½ tsp Chinese five-spice powder

3 tbsp oyster sauce (or vegetarian oyster sauce)

2 tbsp dark soy sauce

2 cloves of garlic, peeled and crushed

8 ready-made bao buns

30g roasted peanuts, roughly chopped

200g sauerkraut

a few coriander leaves

chilli sauce, to serve – I use sriracha

1
Preheat the oven to 240°C/220°C fan/gas 9. Chuck all the mushrooms into a 30x40cm non-stick or lined roasting tin. Add the oil and five-spice powder and toss together. Roast for 20 minutes to start them wilting.

2
Remove the tin from the oven and reduce the temperature to 220°C/200°C fan/gas 7. Give the mushrooms a good mix and return to the oven for 5 to 10 minutes until tender. I like mine to still have a little bite.

3
Meanwhile, whisk together the oyster sauce, dark soy sauce, garlic and 2 tablespoons of water. Pour over the mushrooms, stir together and pop them back in the oven for 2 minutes to warm the sauce. Heat the bao buns according to the packet instructions.

4
Serve everything at the table so you can load up your own buns with the mushrooms, peanuts, sauerkraut, coriander and chilli sauce.

PREP:
8 minutes

COOK:
32 minutes

ISTANBUL EXPRESS BEEF STEW

400g thick-cut sirloin steak

1 red onion, peeled and cut into 1cm pieces

1 red pepper, cut into 1cm pieces

1 tbsp olive oil

2 tomatoes, finely chopped

2 tsp Turkish pepper flakes

1 tsp ground cumin

1 tsp dried oregano

2 tbsp tomato puree or red pepper paste

200ml just-boiled water

20g butter, cut into cubes

a handful of finely chopped parsley leaves

salt and pepper

Turkish cuisine never fails to inspire me, and this speedy stew takes its cue from a traditional dish called *şac tava*. In its classic form, slithers of lamb are fried on a sizzling hot plate with tomatoes, peppers and spices that melt into a sauce. My version is all done in the oven because, let's face it, while cooking on a hot plate over an open fire is a vibe, it doesn't exactly scream midweek meal. By staggering the cooking times, you get the right layers of flavour and a lovely thick sauce for the stew. Serve with nutty bulgur wheat or pillowy soft white bread to make it a hearty meal.

SERVES 2

1
Preheat the oven to 220°C/200°C fan/gas 7. Trim the fat off the steak and cut the meat into 2cm pieces. I find there are always a few fatty pieces of steak around the edge. Don't waste them, instead chuck these into a 24x32cm roasting tin and pop the leaner stuff into a mixing bowl for later.

2
Add the onion and pepper to the roasting tin with the fatty steak, along with the oil and plenty of salt. Mix well and roast for 15 minutes to get some colour on everything.

3
Add the tomatoes, Turkish pepper flakes, cumin, oregano and a pinch of salt and pepper to the roasting in. Mix well and put into the oven for 10 minutes so the tomatoes start to break down.

4
Meanwhile, whisk the tomato puree or red pepper paste with the 200ml just-boiled water and a pinch of salt.

5
Season the lean steak with plenty of salt and pepper and add to the roasting tin. Pour in the tomato sauce and mix well. Dot the butter over the top and return to the oven for 5 to 10 minutes or until the steak is just cooked and still a little pink in the middle. Serve immediately with the parsley scattered over the top.

PREP:
15 minutes

COOK:
35 minutes

CREAMY TAHINI CHICKPEA STEW

2 x 400g tins of chickpeas
1 x 400g tin of chopped tomatoes
1 tbsp tomato puree
2 cloves of garlic, peeled
a 1–2cm piece of fresh ginger, peeled and roughly chopped
1 tsp ground cumin
1 tsp ground coriander
¼ tsp chilli powder – add more if you like it hot
100ml tahini
juice of ½ a lemon
a small handful of coriander leaves
olive oil, for drizzling
salt and pepper

Chickpeas are so wonderfully adaptable. You can roast them until crispy, blitz them until creamy – hummus is one of my all-time favourite things to eat – or use them as a base for this simple stew packed with fragrant spices, garlic and tomatoes. As the chickpeas mellow in the sauce, they absorb all the flavour, and a final drizzle of tahini takes the whole dish to a wonderfully rich creamy place. Using tinned chickpeas makes this accidentally vegan dinner super easy.

SERVES 2

1
Preheat the oven to 200ºC/180ºC fan/gas 6. Drain the chickpeas, reserving the liquid from one of the tins. Pop 100g of chickpeas into a food processor and add 100ml of the chickpea water you reserved. Add the tinned tomatoes, tomato puree, garlic cloves, ginger, cumin, coriander, chilli powder and plenty of salt and pepper. Blitz together until you have a smooth sauce.

2
Chuck the remaining chickpeas into a 24x32cm roasting tin and pour over the sauce you have just made. Swirl 50ml of water around the processor to rinse everything out and tip that into the roasting tray as well. Stir it all together, cover the tin with foil and put into the oven for 20 minutes. Remove the foil and return to the oven for 10 to 15 minutes until the top is all bubbling.

3
Meanwhile, whisk the tahini together with 100ml of water, the lemon juice and a pinch of salt until creamy. Pour into the chickpeas and stir together. Scatter over the coriander and serve immediately with a drizzle of olive oil.

PREP:
10 minutes

COOK:
35 minutes

NEXT-LEVEL CHORIZO SHAKSHUKA

100g chorizo, finely chopped
1 red onion, peeled and finely chopped
2 tsp olive oil
2 cloves of garlic, peeled and crushed
1 x 400g tin of chopped tomatoes
1 tsp smoked paprika, plus extra to serve
½ tsp chilli flakes
4 medium free-range eggs
optional: 1 tbsp tahini, for drizzling
a small handful of finely chopped parsley leaves
salt and pepper

Now one of my go-to recipes for brunch or a quick and easy dinner, a traybake shakshuka became a lifesaver when I was cooking brunch for my huge family on one of our annual weekends away. It's far easier to cook a shak for twenty people in the oven than to juggle multiple frying pans on the hob. This method works so brilliantly that I use it when I'm making a quick bite for me and my partner. If you're cooking for four, simply double the ingredients and grab yourself a larger roasting tin. The tahini at the end is the chef's kiss, luxing it up and making it feel even more indulgent. Give it a whirl – you won't regret it!

SERVES 2

1
Preheat the oven to 220°C/200°C fan/gas 7. Chuck the chorizo, red onion, olive oil and a pinch of salt into a 24x32cm roasting tin. Toss together and roast for 10 to 12 minutes to get some colour on to everything.

2
Add the garlic straight into the roasting tin and mix together. Pour in the tinned tomatoes and add the paprika, chilli flakes and a good pinch of salt and pepper. Stir together and return to the oven for 5 minutes to warm the sauce through.

3
Remove the tin from the oven and reduce the temperature to 200°C/180°C fan/gas 6. Crack the eggs into the sauce and return to the oven for 4 to 6 minutes or until the whites have set. Drizzle over the tahini, if using, and scatter over the parsley. Serve immediately with an extra pinch of smoked paprika if you like.

PREP:
10 minutes

COOK:
23 minutes

MOROCCAN-STYLE CREAMY COCONUT LENTIL SOUP

200g red lentils
1 x 400g tin of chopped tomatoes
1 x 400ml tin of coconut milk
300ml just-boiled water
2 tsp ras el hanout
2 tsp garlic powder
1 tsp ground ginger
juice of ½ a lemon
a small handful of coriander leaves
optional: chilli oil, for drizzling
salt and pepper

Whenever you're craving a warm, comforting food hug, this soup is exactly what you need in your life. Creamy and reassuringly thick, it's reminiscent of a hearty Indian or Sri Lankan dhal but infused with Moroccan flavours: warming ground ginger and ras el hanout, a North African spice mix that really packs a punch. Cooking-wise it's fabulously fuss-free. Just hurl everything into the oven and let it do all the hard work for you.

SERVES 2

1
Preheat the oven to 220°C/200°C fan/gas 7. Chuck the lentils, tomatoes, coconut milk, 300ml just-boiled water, ras el hanout, garlic powder, ground ginger and a good pinch of salt and pepper into a 24x32cm roasting tin. Mix well and cover the tin with foil. Put into the oven for 30 to 35 minutes or until the lentils are cooked through.

2
Stir in the lemon juice and check the seasoning, adding salt to taste. Once it's perfect, serve with plenty of coriander and a drizzle of chilli oil, if you fancy.

PREP:
5 minutes

COOK:
35 minutes

COCONUT, CORIANDER
AND LIME COD

- 4 cod fillets (500–600g in total)
- 2 limes – 1 zested and then sliced, ½ juiced, and ½ cut into little wedges
- a handful of finely chopped coriander leaves
- 1 x 400g tin of coconut milk
- 2 tbsp fish sauce
- 2 cloves of garlic, peeled and grated
- a 1–2cm piece of fresh ginger, peeled and grated
- 1 tsp turmeric
- crispy chilli oil, for drizzling
- salt

There is something so magnificent about this effortless traybake. Cod fillets gently poach in creamy coconut milk, infused with lime, coriander, ginger and garlic. Like the perfect partnership, these ingredients give back, infusing the cod with incredible flavour. It's easy, elegant cooking. When it's time to serve, I simply must have plenty of rice and a solid drizzle of chilli oil over my fish. My go-to is Lao Gan Ma crispy chilli oil. You can find it in most Asian grocery stores or larger supermarkets. Spoiler alert: once you start, you can't stop – it's literally amazing.

SERVES 4

1
Preheat the oven to 200°C/180°C fan/gas 6. Pat the cod dry and season both sides with salt.

2
Put the lime slices into the bottom of a 24x32cm roasting tin and place the fish on top. Scatter over the coriander.

3
Whisk together the coconut milk, fish sauce, garlic, ginger, turmeric and the lime zest and juice. Pour over the fish and cover the roasting tin with foil. Roast in the oven for 20 to 25 minutes or until the cod is just cooked through.

4
Transfer the cod to four serving bowls. Give the sauce a good mix so it's lovely and smooth and spoon generously over the fish. Drizzle over some chilli oil and serve immediately with the little lime wedges on the side. This goes beautifully with rice or noodles.

PREP:
10 minutes

COOK:
25 minutes

MELTED LEEKS
WITH GARLICKY YOGHURT AND CHILLI BUTTER

800g trimmed leeks, finely sliced

4 cloves of garlic, peeled – 3 finely chopped and 1 crushed

2 tbsp olive oil

250ml just-boiled water

3 tbsp tomato puree or red pepper paste

300g Greek yoghurt at room temperature – I use 10% fat

40g butter

1½ tsp Turkish pepper flakes

a small handful of finely chopped parsley leaves

salt and pepper

When you roast leeks en masse, they go soft and sweet, almost melting, and here they're soaking up the added flavours of garlic and tomato. Any little bits that stray from the pack go really crispy and smoky in the oven. This is already such a taste sensation, but why not take it even further and serve with thick creamy yoghurt and a decadent drizzle of chilli butter? The combination of the hot silky leeks melting into the yoghurt is just divine.

SERVES 2 AS A MAIN

1
Preheat the oven to 240°C/220°C fan/gas 9. Chuck the leeks into a 30x40cm non-stick or lined baking tray and add the finely chopped garlic, olive oil and plenty of salt and pepper. Toss together.

2
Whisk the 250ml just-boiled water with 2 tablespoons of the tomato puree or red pepper paste. Pour over the leeks and stir together. Put into the oven and roast for 15 to 20 minutes or until the leeks are soft and a little charred on top. Give them a good mix and check the seasoning, adding salt to taste.

3
Meanwhile, stir the final clove of crushed garlic and a pinch of salt into the yoghurt.

4
Melt the butter in little saucepan over a medium heat. Turn off the heat and add the Turkish pepper flakes and a pinch of salt. Swirl together, then add the final 1 tablespoon of tomato puree or red pepper paste. It will split as you mix, so whisk in 1–2 tablespoons of water to help it come back together.

5
Load the leeks on to two serving plates and dollop the yoghurt over each one. Spoon over the chilli butter and serve immediately with a little parsley scattered over the top.

PREP:
15 minutes

COOK:
20 minutes

CREAMY THAI PEANUT CHICKEN CURRY	58
THE GREATEST CHICKEN SHAWARMA SALAD	60
CRINKLE-TOP CHICKEN AND BACON PIE	62
ELEKTRA'S GREEK CHICKEN TRAYBAKE	64
CHICKEN AND AUBERGINE BULGUR PILAF	66
SLOW-COOKED BUTTER CHICKEN	68
FETA-LICIOUS CHICKEN MEATBALLS	70
SEOULFUL KOREAN GARLIC CHICKEN	72
PADRÓN PEPPER AND CHORIZO CHICKEN BAKE	74
TANDOORI ROAST CHICKEN RICE	76
MY QUICK-COOK CHICKEN ADOBO	78
SAFFRON AND PRESERVED LEMON TAGINE TRAYBAKE	80
ROASTED CAJUN CHICKEN WITH AVOCADO SOURED CREAM	82
CREAMY CHIPOTLE CHICKEN ORZO	84
GEORGIAN-STYLE CHICKEN	86
DREAMY CREAMY CHICKEN PASTA BAKE	88
PERSIAN-STYLE SAFFRON CHICKEN RICE	90
SPEEDY CHICKEN KORMA	92
SUMAC-SPICED CHICKEN WITH CARAMELIZED ONIONS	94
CHEESY CHICKEN MELTS	96
BAHARAT-SPICED CHICKEN AND SWEET POTATO WEDGES	98

CHICKEN RECIPES

I couldn't imagine writing this cookbook without dedicating a whole chapter to chicken. After all, who doesn't love a good chicken traybake? They are the ultimate crowd-pleaser! With over twenty irresistible recipes, you'll find everything from quick and fuss-free options for busy days to slow-cooked roast dinners and elegant dishes that are perfect for impressing guests.

CREAMY THAI PEANUT CHICKEN CURRY

600g chicken breasts, sliced into 1cm strips

2 tbsp Thai red curry paste – I use Mae Ploy

150g tenderstem broccoli

1 red onion, peeled and sliced into ½cm half-moons

1 red pepper, sliced into 1cm strips

2 tbsp groundnut oil

400ml coconut milk

2 tbsp smooth peanut butter

2 tbsp fish sauce

juice of ½ a lime

15g roasted peanuts

1 red chilli, finely sliced

a few Thai basil leaves or coriander leaves

This is one of my favourite dinners after a long day. It's simple but packed with flavour. To nail it, I roast off the chicken and veggies to intensify their flavours. While that happens, I get the sauce bubbling on the stove, letting it thicken beautifully. If you did this all together, everything would steam in the oven and you would end up with a watery curry. For me that's a big no-no – I like a thick curry sauce. You can serve this with your choice of rice or noodles.

SERVES 4

1
Preheat the oven to 200°C/180°C fan/gas 6. Chuck the chicken into a bowl and add 1 tablespoon of the curry paste. Mix well and transfer to a 30x40cm roasting tin. Add the broccoli, red onion and pepper. Pour over the oil and toss together. Roast for 10 minutes to get everything going.

2
Meanwhile, pour the coconut milk into a saucepan and add the final 1 tablespoon of curry paste, peanut butter, fish sauce and lime juice. Whisk together and bring to the boil over a medium-high heat. Let it bubble away, stirring occasionally, while the chicken cooks. You want to reduce it as much as possible to avoid a watery sauce.

3
Pour the sauce over the chicken and return to the oven for 10 to 15 minutes or until the chicken is cooked through and tender. Scatter over the peanuts, chilli and Thai basil or coriander, and serve immediately.

PREP:
12 minutes

COOK:
25 minutes

THE GREATEST CHICKEN SHAWARMA SALAD

for the chicken:
600g boneless skinless chicken thigh fillets, cut into 1cm strips
juice of ½ a lemon
2 tbsp mayonnaise
1 tbsp tomato puree
1 tbsp groundnut or neutral oil
2 tsp baharat
1 tsp Turkish pepper flakes
1 tsp sumac, plus extra to serve
salt and pepper

for the dressing:
180g soured cream
2 cloves of garlic, peeled and crushed

for the salad:
2 romaine hearts, roughly chopped
2 large tomatoes, roughly chopped
1 cucumber, sliced into half-moons
100g pitted olives, roughly chopped
30 pickled jalapeños, finely chopped
juice of ½ a lemon
1 tbsp olive oil

Every now and then I get completely obsessed with a recipe and I can't stop making it, and this is one of those. Say hello to the most delicious, juicy chicken dish you'll ever cook. The secret lies in the marinade: a fragrant blend of shawarma spices like baharat and sumac, all bound together with everyone's favourite – mayonnaise. Yes, mayo! While it might sound unconventional, it works wonders, taking the place of yoghurt to make the chicken irresistibly juicy and velvety as it roasts. It's so versatile – you can toss it into this wonderful salad, slap it into a wrap or serve it with buttery rice. The leftovers heat up beautifully and make the ultimate sandwich filling. Trust me, you're going to love it.

SERVES 4

1
Preheat the oven to 220°C/200°C fan/gas 7. Chuck the chicken into a mixing bowl and add the lemon juice, mayonnaise, tomato puree, oil, baharat, Turkish pepper flakes, sumac and a heavy pinch of salt and pepper. Mix well and transfer to a 30x40cm non-stick or lined roasting tin. Spread out into an even layer and roast in the oven for 18 to 20 minutes or until cooked through, a little charred and super juicy.

2
Meanwhile, mix the soured cream together with the garlic and a pinch of salt.

3
Put the romaine hearts, tomatoes, cucumber, olives, jalapeños, lemon juice, olive oil and a pinch of salt into a massive mixing bowl and toss together.

4
To serve, divide the salad between four serving bowls. Mix the chicken in the roasting juices and top each bowl with a big pile of meat, spooning over any remaining juices. Drizzle over the dressing and add a pinch of sumac to each.

PREP:
20 minutes

COOK:
20 minutes

CRINKLE-TOP CHICKEN AND BACON PIE

- 1kg boneless skinless chicken thigh fillets, cut into 2–3cm pieces
- 200g lardons or bacon
- 2 sprigs of thyme, leaves picked
- 1 tbsp olive oil
- 300ml double cream
- 2 tsp Dijon mustard
- 2 cloves of garlic, peeled and crushed
- 3 tbsp plain flour
- 6 spring onions, finely chopped
- 270g pack filo pastry (7 sheets) – I use Jus-Rol
- 1 free-range egg, whisked
- salt and pepper

If I had to showcase the magic of traybake cooking, this chicken pie would be the ultimate example. It's an effortless but ever-so-indulgent creamy chicken pie, with a lovely thick sauce, flavoured with smoky bacon and thyme. The top is studded with filo pastry that you deliberately scrunch up by hand so it goes all spiky and crispy in the oven. It's simple to prepare and guaranteed to impress.

SERVES 6

1
Preheat the oven to 200°C/180°C fan/gas 6. Chuck the chicken, lardons or bacon and thyme leaves into a 24x32cm roasting tin. Add the oil and plenty of salt and pepper. Mix well and roast for 25 minutes to get some colour on to the chicken.

2
Meanwhile, whisk together the double cream, Dijon mustard, garlic and plenty of salt and pepper.

3
Remove the chicken from the oven and scatter over the flour. Mix well to coat each piece. Add the spring onions, pour over the cream sauce and stir together.

4
Tear each piece of filo pastry in half and scrunch each half into a jaggedy-looking ball. Starting at one corner of the pie, place the scrunched-up filo on top of the chicken filling. Keep going with more scrunched-up pieces of pastry until the whole pie is covered in a very spiky, punk-rock topping. Gently brush with the egg and pop it back into the oven for 20 minutes or until the pastry is all golden and the filling thick and rich. Leave to rest for 5 to 10 minutes before serving. This pairs perfectly with buttery mash and a green salad.

PREP:
15 minutes

COOK:
45 minutes

ELEKTRA'S GREEK CHICKEN TRAYBAKE

2 tbsp olive oil

zest and juice of 1 lemon

4 cloves of garlic, peeled and crushed

2 tbsp yellow mustard

2 tsp smoked paprika

2 tsp dried oregano

4 chicken legs, skin on and bone in (about 1kg in total)

800g potatoes, cut into little wedges – I halve them and then cut each half into thirds

300ml white wine or hot chicken stock – from 1 stock cube

salt and pepper

This is a very simple Greek traybake, the classic combo of chicken and potatoes in a glorious garlicky lemon marinade. I picked up the recipe from a wonderful lady called Elektra, who was the cook in a house I was staying at during one of my annual summer trips to Greece. It's easy cooking. The oven does all the hard work for you, crisping up the chicken to that finger-licking stage and giving the potatoes time to drink up all the punchy flavours in the roasting tin.

SERVES 4

1
Preheat the oven to 220ºC/200ºC fan/gas 7. Mix the olive oil, lemon zest and juice, garlic, mustard, paprika, oregano and loads of salt and pepper into a dressing.

2
Chuck the chicken and potatoes into a 30x40cm roasting tin and pour over the dressing. Toss together and pour in the wine or chicken stock. Scrunch up some baking paper and wet it under the cold tap. Spread this over the chicken and potatoes and tuck in the sides. Cover the whole tray with foil and roast in the oven for 30 minutes. Remove the foil and the baking paper and roast for 40 to 45 minutes or until everything is golden and crispy. Serve immediately.

PREP:
10 minutes

COOK:
1 hour 15 minutes

CHICKEN AND AUBERGINE BULGUR PILAF

1 onion, peeled and finely chopped

2 aubergines, cut into 1–2cm pieces

3 tbsp olive oil

350ml hot chicken stock – from 1 stock cube

1 tbsp pomegranate molasses

2 tsp garlic powder

2 tsp baharat

1 tsp dried thyme

1 kg chicken thighs, skin on and bone in

200g bulgur wheat

juice of ½ a lemon, plus wedges to serve

a large handful of finely chopped parsley leaves

30g walnuts

salt and pepper

PREP:
15 minutes

COOK:
1 hour 10 minutes

I'm a huge fan of oven-baking chicken thighs with bulgur wheat. The robust grains soften alongside the chicken, soaking up all those comforting juices. To make this dish feel super sophisticated, I have flavoured it with tangy pomegranate molasses, aromatic baharat and a herbal hit of thyme. For a rather cheffy finish, I give a final flourish of microplaned walnuts right into the bulgur. This gives an instant creaminess and rich flavour, without the crunch. I love it, and it looks super impressive served in a huge dish at the table.

SERVES 4

1
Preheat the oven to 200°C/180°C fan/gas 6. Put the onion and aubergines into a 30x40cm roasting tin. Add 2 tablespoons of the oil and a good pinch of salt and pepper. Toss together.

2
Whisk together the stock, pomegranate molasses, garlic powder, 1 teaspoon of baharat, thyme and a good pinch of salt and pepper.

3
Chuck the chicken into a mixing bowl and add the last 1 tablespoon of oil and the last 1 teaspoon of baharat. Add plenty of salt and pepper and toss together.

4
Scatter the bulgur wheat into the roasting tin with the vegetables and pour over the stock. Arrange the chicken over the top and cover with foil. Put into the oven and roast for 25 minutes to get some heat into everything. Remove the foil and return to the oven for 40 to 45 minutes or until the chicken is cooked through and golden and the bulgur really soft.

5
Remove the chicken from the roasting tin and set to one side. Add the lemon juice, most of the parsley and then microplane most of the walnuts into the roasting tin. If you don't have a microplane, just chop the walnuts into a fine rubble and scatter them over at the end. Mix well and check the seasoning, adding salt and pepper to taste. Transfer to a serving dish and place the chicken on top. Scatter over the remaining parsley and microplane the remaining walnuts over the top. Serve immediately with lemon wedges on the side.

SLOW-COOKED BUTTER CHICKEN

2 onions, peeled and roughly sliced
1 tbsp groundnut or neutral oil
1 x 400g tin of chopped tomatoes
2 tbsp tomato puree
6 cloves of garlic, peeled and crushed
a 2–3cm piece of fresh ginger, peeled and grated
2 tsp garam masala
1 tsp ground cumin
1 tsp Kashmiri chilli powder
½ tsp ground cinnamon
600g boneless skinless chicken thigh fillets, cut into 5cm pieces
250ml just-boiled water
120ml double cream
35g butter, cubed
a pinch of dried fenugreek leaves
salt

PREP:
15 minutes

COOK:
1 hour 40 minutes

Sunday curry night has been a cherished family tradition for years, and nothing beats a truly knockout butter chicken. The spices melt into a rich, creamy sauce, making it the ultimate comfort food classic. Alongside lashings of butter, the real star here is fenugreek, a spice that smells like curry itself. I love using dried fenugreek leaves, which are fantastic if you can find them. If not, ground fenugreek works just as well – just add ¼ of a teaspoon with the other spices. Another favourite Indian spice of mine is Kashmiri chilli powder. It's not too spicy but offers a smoky depth and a stunning red hue. I don't want to put any of you guys off making this lush recipe, so if you can't get hold of it, swap it out for 1 teaspoon of paprika and some chilli powder.

SERVES 4

1
Preheat the oven to 200°C/180°C fan/gas 6. Chuck the onions into a 24x32cm roasting tin and add the oil and a good pinch of salt. Toss together and pour in 3 tablespoons of water. Pop into the oven for 20 minutes to get some colour on them.

2
Meanwhile, mix the tinned tomatoes, tomato puree, garlic, ginger, garam masala, cumin, Kashmiri chilli powder, cinnamon and a really good pinch of salt together.

3
Reduce the oven temperature to 180°C/160°C fan/gas 4. Transfer the chicken to the tray with the onions. Add the sauce and 250ml just-boiled water and mix well. Scrunch up some baking paper and spread it over the chicken, then cover the whole tray with foil. Bake for 30 minutes in the oven to cook the chicken.

4
Remove the foil and baking paper from the tray. Pour in the cream, add the butter and mix well. Make sure the chicken is covered in the sauce – you can use a spoon to push it down. Return the tin to the oven for 40 to 50 minutes or until the sauce is all bubbling and thick.

5
Crush a big pinch of fenugreek leaves between your hands, straight into the curry, and stir. Check the seasoning, adding salt to taste, and serve immediately. I would always have fluffy rice on the side, and, if you're feeling decadent, buttery naan.

FETA-LICIOUS CHICKEN MEATBALLS

for the meatballs:
- 600g chicken breasts or minced chicken
- 150g feta
- 50g black pitted olives
- 4 spring onions, roughly chopped
- 2 cloves of garlic, peeled
- 2 tbsp tomato puree
- 2 tsp Turkish pepper flakes
- 1 tsp dried oregano
- salt and pepper

for the sauce:
- 680g tomato passata
- 2 tsp Turkish pepper flakes
- 2 tsp dried oregano
- 1 tsp garlic powder
- 50g feta
- a small handful of finely chopped parsley leaves

I am a big fan of chicken meatballs. They are juicy and light and super easy to make. These ones are flavoured with feta, olives and Turkish pepper flakes, and then cooked in a rich tomato sauce. You can serve them with salad, pasta or a jacket potato, and they are epic the next day for a simple lunch al desko in the office.

SERVES 4

1
Preheat the oven to 200°C/180°C fan/gas 6. To make the meatballs, chuck the chicken breasts or mince into a food processor and add the remaining meatball ingredients and a pinch of salt and pepper. Blitz until smooth and roll into 16 meatballs.

2
Swirl a few tablespoons of the passata around the base of a 24x32cm roasting tin. Mix the rest of the passata with the Turkish pepper flakes, dried oregano, garlic powder and big pinch of salt and pepper.

3
Arrange the meatballs in the roasting tin and pour over the sauce so they are covered. Put into the oven for 12 to 15 minutes or until the meatballs are cooked through. You can cut one in half to test if it's cooked – it will be pale in colour and firm-textured all the way though. If it's not quite there, return the tin to the oven for a few minutes more until they are perfectly cooked all the way though.

4
Crumble the remaining 50g of feta cheese over the top and scatter over the parsley. Serve immediately.

PREP:
15 minutes

COOK:
15 minutes

SEOULFUL KOREAN GARLIC CHICKEN

- 4 tbsp gochujang paste
- 2 tbsp dark soy sauce
- 3 tbsp rice wine
- 1 tbsp sesame oil
- 1 tsp caster sugar
- a 4–5cm piece of fresh ginger, peeled and grated
- 1kg chicken thighs, skin on and bone in
- 250ml hot chicken stock – from 1 stock cube
- 2 onions, peeled and roughly chopped
- 8 cloves of garlic, peeled
- 650g new potatoes, halved, larger ones cut into thirds
- 4 spring onions, finely sliced
- 2 tsp toasted sesame seeds

This is my take on *dak-dori-tang*, a Korean chicken and potato stew, reimagined as a quick and easy traybake. It's absolutely packed with flavour, thanks to a lip-smacking sauce made from gochujang paste, vinegar and soy sauce. Chicken thighs and onions roast together with little new potatoes that soak up every drop of that rich, deeply savoury sauce. Gochujang paste is now widely available in most supermarkets. I love using a mild one by Sun Hee, but feel free to choose your favourite.

SERVES 4

1
Preheat the oven to 220°C/200°C fan/gas 7. Whisk together the gochujang, soy sauce, rice wine, sesame oil, sugar and ginger in a jug.

2
Chuck the chicken into a mixing bowl, spoon over 3 tablespoons of the sauce you have just made and mix well.

3
Pour the stock into the jug with the remaining sauce and whisk together.

4
Put the onions, garlic cloves, potatoes and chicken into a 30x40cm roasting tin. Pour over the stock. Cover with foil and cook for 30 minutes. Remove the foil and reduce the temperature to 200°C/180°C fan/gas 6. Return the tin to the oven and roast for 30 to 40 minutes or until the chicken is lovely and crispy and the tops of the potatoes golden. Scatter over the spring onions and sesame seeds and serve immediately.

PREP:
10 minutes

COOK:
1 hour 10 minutes

PADRÓN PEPPER AND CHORIZO CHICKEN BAKE

- 500g cherry tomatoes, halved
- 180g Padrón peppers
- 100g chorizo, finely chopped into 0.5cm cubes
- 6 cloves of garlic, peeled and roughly sliced
- a handful of roughly chopped parsley leaves, plus extra to garnish
- zest and juice of ½ a lemon
- 2 tbsp olive oil
- 2 tsp smoked paprika
- 2 tsp dried oregano
- 1 tsp ground cumin
- 600g chicken breasts, cut into 2–3cm pieces
- 1 x 400g tin of cannellini beans, drained and rinsed
- 180ml white wine
- salt and pepper

This dish is the ultimate week-night warrior – big on flavour, low on effort. Inspired by Spanish ingredients, it features a rich, smoky sauce made with tomatoes, smoked paprika, chorizo and garlic. It's hearty and satisfying, thanks to the addition of tender chicken, beans and – another win – my favourite Padrón peppers. They taste so good and cook much faster than regular peppers, meaning this lush dinner is ready in under an hour.

SERVES 4

1
Preheat the oven to 200°C/180°C fan/gas 6. Chuck the tomatoes, Padrón peppers, chorizo, garlic, parsley, lemon zest and juice, olive oil and a good pinch of salt and pepper into a 30x40cm roasting tin. Then add 1 teaspoon of the smoked paprika, 1 teaspoon of the oregano and half a teaspoon of the cumin. Toss together and put into the oven to roast for 20 minutes.

2
Meanwhile, put the chicken into a mixing bowl and add the remaining 1 teaspoon of smoked paprika, 1 teaspoon of oregano and the other half a teaspoon of cumin. Add a good pinch of salt and pepper and mix well.

3
Tip the chicken and cannellini beans into the tray with the veg, mix well and pour in the wine. Scrunch up a piece of baking paper large enough to cover the roasting tin and wet it under the cold tap. Spread it out over the chicken and tuck in the sides. Roast for 18 to 20 minutes or until the chicken is cooked through and juicy. Scatter over a little extra parsley and serve immediately.

PREP:
15 minutes

COOK:
40 minutes

TANDOORI ROAST CHICKEN RICE

3 onions, peeled and roughly sliced into rings
1 tbsp olive oil
100g butter, at room temperature
2 tsp garam masala
1 tsp ground cumin
1 tsp mild chilli powder
½ tsp turmeric
6 cloves of garlic, peeled and crushed
a 4–5cm piece of fresh ginger, peeled and grated
1 whole chicken (approx. 2kg), at room temperature
150ml white wine
300g basmati rice
500ml hot chicken stock – from 1 stock cube
lemon wedges, to serve
salt and pepper

PREP:
20 minutes

COOK:
2 hours

This is such a sexy spin on the classic roast chicken, slathering the bird in an Indian-inspired spiced butter packed with garlic and ginger. As the chicken roasts, the butter melts, flavouring the meat and keeping it irresistibly juicy. The spices enhance the charred, crispy skin, while the buttery, wine-infused juices create a delicious base for flavourful rice that absorbs all that unctuous goodness in the oven. It's truly perfection. I love serving the chicken and rice with hot lime pickle and a side of crunchy vegetables for balance. For the best results, take the chicken out of the fridge a few hours before cooking to bring it to room temperature. This prevents the exterior from overcooking and drying out while ensuring the centre cooks through beautifully.

SERVES 4–6

1
Preheat the oven to 220°C/200°C fan/gas 7. Pop the onions into a 24x32cm roasting tin. Drizzle over the oil and season with salt and pepper.

2
Mix the butter with the garam masala, cumin, chilli powder, turmeric, garlic, ginger, a massive pinch of salt and a little pepper.

3
Pat the chicken dry and squish most of the butter under the skin that's above the breasts. Slather the remaining butter all over the chicken. Place on the onions and season the top with a little salt. Pour in the wine and roast in the oven for 1¼ to 1½ hours or until the chicken is cooked through and the juices run clear. Put the chicken on to a warm plate, cover and leave to rest for 15 minutes before carving, then cover again until ready to serve.

4
Meanwhile, reduce the oven temperature to 200°C/180°C fan/gas 6. Add the rice to the roasting tin and mix it into all the juices. Pour in the stock and stir it all together. Cover with foil and put into the oven for 15 minutes. Remove the foil and cook for a further 10 to 15 minutes or until the rice is cooked and the edges are a little crispy.

5
Tip any of the resting juices into the rice and mix with a fork. Check the seasoning, adding salt to taste. Serve immediately with the chicken and plenty of lemon wedges.

MY QUICK-COOK CHICKEN ADOBO

600g boneless skinless chicken thigh fillets, cut into 2cm strips

2 tbsp dark soy sauce, plus extra to serve

2 tbsp white wine vinegar

4 cloves of garlic, peeled and crushed

2 tsp ground black pepper

3 tsp light brown sugar

4 fresh bay leaves

2 onions, peeled and finely sliced

2 tbsp groundnut or neutral oil

200ml hot chicken stock – from ½ a stock cube

4 spring onions, finely sliced

salt

One of the world's most incredible chicken dishes is the Filipino classic *adobo*. Juicy chicken thighs are braised to perfection in a soy sauce infused with fragrant bay leaves and black peppercorns. Inspired by this joyous recipe, I've created a traybake version that's just as rich and tangy as the original. The chicken gets slightly charred on top but stays super juicy and wonderfully perfumed from the bay leaves. To do this knockout dish justice, skip flavourless dried bay leaves and use fresh ones.

SERVES 4

1
Preheat the oven to 220°C/200°C fan/gas 7. Pop the chicken into a shallow dish and add the soy sauce, vinegar, garlic, black pepper, sugar and 2 tablespoons of water. Rub the bay leaves between your hands to release their oils and add them as well. Mix well, cover and leave to marinate for 30 minutes.

2
While that's happening, chuck the onions, oil and a tiny pinch of salt into a 24x32cm roasting tin. Toss together and roast for 10 to 15 minutes to get some char into the onions.

3
Add the chicken to the roasting tin with the onions. Swirl the stock around the marinating dish and empty it into the roasting tin so that none of the flavours are left behind. Return the tin to the oven for 20 to 25 minutes or until the chicken is cooked through and a little charred and you have a lovely sauce. Scatter over the spring onions and serve immediately with soy sauce to taste. I like this with mountains of fluffy rice.

PREP:
15 minutes

MARINATE:
30 minutes

COOK:
40 minutes

SAFFRON AND PRESERVED LEMON TAGINE TRAYBAKE

- a pinch of saffron
- 2 tbsp just-boiled water
- 2 preserved lemons, deseeded and roughly chopped
- a large handful of coriander, leaves and stalks, plus a few extra leaves, to garnish
- 4 cloves of garlic, peeled
- 2 tsp paprika
- 1 tsp ground ginger
- 2 tbsp olive oil
- 1 kg chicken thighs, skin on and bone in
- 2 onions, peeled and finely sliced
- 300ml hot chicken stock – from 1 stock cube
- 100g pitted green olives
- salt and pepper

This easy chicken traybake is flavoured with some of my favourite Moroccan ingredients including sunshine-yellow saffron, perfumed preserved lemons and warming ground ginger. These big flavours marry together with the joyous chicken juices and melting soft onions to create a magnificent sauce that's both comforting and complex. Pair it with buttery couscous to soak up every last drop of this divine dish.

SERVES 4

1
Preheat the oven to 200°C/180°C fan/gas 6. Put the saffron into a little dish and add the just-boiled water. Stir and leave to infuse for a few minutes.

2
Put the preserved lemons, coriander, garlic cloves, paprika, ginger, olive oil and a big pinch of salt and pepper into a mini chopper. Pour in the saffron water and blitz into a smooth paste.

3
Pop the chicken into a 24x32cm roasting tin and add the spice paste. Mix well, really massaging it into the thighs. Add the onions. Mix well again and arrange the chicken thighs skin side up. Pour in the stock. Scrunch up some baking paper and spread it over the chicken. Cover the whole tray with foil and roast in the oven for 1 hour to let the flavours develop and the chicken cook.

4
Remove the foil and baking paper and scatter the olives over the chicken. Shake the roasting tin so they sink into the juices. Return to the oven for 20 to 25 minutes or until the chicken skin is nice and golden. Scatter over a few coriander leaves and serve immediately.

PREP:
15 minutes

COOK:
1 hour 25 minutes

ROASTED CAJUN CHICKEN
WITH AVOCADO SOURED CREAM

700g new potatoes, halved, larger ones cut into thirds

1 kg chicken thighs, skin on and bone in

2 red peppers, roughly chopped

2 tbsp olive oil

2 tsp garlic powder

1 tbsp Cajun seasoning – I use Schwartz

200ml white wine or hot chicken stock – from ½ a stock cube

1 large ripe avocado

100g soured cream

juice of ½ a lime

a handful of finely chopped coriander leaves

salt and pepper

This is such a wonderful low-rent dinner, using the classic combo of chicken thighs and potatoes. This version is slathered in Cajun seasoning, which, when you bung it in the oven with a splash of white wine, gives you the most perfect crispy chicken and a flavourful sauce to spoon over the top. On its own, it's already a winner, but trust me, it's even better with a dollop of avocado soured cream on the side.

SERVES 4

1
Preheat the oven to 200ºC/180ºC fan/gas 6. Chuck the potatoes into a 30x40cm roasting tin.

2
Add the chicken thighs and peppers. Pour in the oil and add the garlic powder and plenty of salt and pepper. Mix well so everything gets seasoned and arrange the chicken skin side up. Sprinkle over the Cajun seasoning, making sure you get plenty on the chicken skin. Give the tray a good jiggle so everything is spread out evenly and pour in the wine or stock. Roast for 50 to 60 minutes or until everything is golden and cooked through.

3
Meanwhile, mash the avocado in a mixing bowl until smooth. Add the soured cream, lime juice, coriander and a pinch of salt. Mix well and serve immediately with the chicken – and don't forget to spoon over all those lush juices from the roasting tin.

PREP:
15 minutes

COOK:
1 hour

CREAMY CHIPOTLE CHICKEN ORZO

- 1 tbsp chipotle chilli paste – I use Gran Luchito
- 750ml hot chicken stock – from 1 stock cube
- 400g orzo
- 500g chicken breasts, cut into 1cm strips
- 2 tsp garlic powder
- 1 tsp smoked paprika
- 1 tsp dried oregano
- 100ml double cream
- 100ml just-boiled water
- 50g Parmesan cheese, plus extra to serve
- salt and pepper

Grab yourself a spoon and sink into this dreamy chicken orzo traybake. It's got all the trappings that ridiculously good comfort food should have – pasta, cheese and cream – but with a bold, smoky kick from the chipotle chilli paste that keeps it interesting. The orzo works so well, soaking up all the flavours as it cooks. Then, a little like a risotto, you finish it off with just enough liquid and a mountain of cheese so that it goes uber oozy and utterly satisfying.

SERVES 4

1
Preheat the oven to 200ºC/180ºC fan/gas 6. Whisk the chipotle chilli paste together with the stock and a pinch of salt and pepper.

2
Chuck the orzo into a 24x32cm roasting tin and pour over the stock. Cover with foil and put into the oven for 10 minutes so the orzo can start cooking.

3
Meanwhile, pop the chicken into a mixing bowl and add the garlic powder, smoked paprika, oregano and a good pinch of salt and pepper. Mix well and tip into the roasting tin with the orzo. Stir together and replace the foil. Return to the oven for 10 minutes until the chicken is almost cooked through.

4
Pour the double cream into the roasting tin, add 50ml of just-boiled water and mix well. Cover again with foil and return to the oven for 8 to 10 minutes or until the chicken is cooked through.

5
Add plenty of Parm and another 50ml of just-boiled water to the orzo. Mix everything together until it's wonderfully creamy. Check the seasoning, adding salt to taste, and then serve immediately with more Parm at the table.

PREP:
10 minutes

COOK:
30 minutes

GEORGIAN-STYLE CHICKEN

- 2 onions, peeled and finely sliced
- 4 cloves of garlic, peeled and finely chopped
- a large handful of finely chopped coriander leaves
- 1 x 400g tin of chopped tomatoes
- 2 tbsp tomato puree
- 50g walnuts, finely chopped
- 2 tsp Turkish pepper flakes
- 2 tsp ground coriander
- ½ tsp ground fenugreek
- 300ml hot chicken stock – from 1 stock cube
- 1kg chicken thighs, skin on and bone in
- 2 red peppers, sliced into 2–3cm strips
- salt and pepper

This heavenly chicken traybake takes inspiration from the sumptuous Georgian dish *chakhokhbili*, a rich, herb-laden tomato stew. While I must confess that I've never had the pleasure of visiting Georgia, I've long admired its vibrant cuisine from afar. If anyone wants to bring me a plate of *khinkali* (Georgian meat dumplings), I am available any time. With this recipe, I've borrowed elements to make something more accessible in my own kitchen. Everything roasts together, the chicken absorbing the flavour of the tomatoes, walnuts, fenugreek and sweet peppers. The result is a dish that's unexpectedly familiar, wonderfully fragrant and completely irresistible.

SERVES 4

1
Preheat the oven to 200°C/180°C fan/gas 6. Pop the onions into a 30x40cm roasting tin. Add the garlic, coriander, chopped tomatoes, tomato puree, walnuts, Turkish pepper flakes, ground coriander, fenugreek, stock and plenty of salt and pepper. Mix well.

2
Season the chicken with loads of salt and pepper, then put it into the roasting tin. Add the peppers and mix everything together, then arrange the chicken so it's skin side up. Scrunch up some baking paper, then spread it over the chicken and veg and tuck in the sides. Put the tin into the oven to roast for 1 hour until the meat is cooked, then remove the baking paper and return to the oven for 15 to 20 minutes or until the chicken is golden on top. I love this with bulgur wheat or couscous and green beans.

PREP:
10 minutes

COOK:
1 hour 20 minutes

DREAMY CREAMY CHICKEN PASTA BAKE

6 tomatoes, roughly chopped (about 450g in total)

4 cloves of garlic, peeled

1 onion, peeled and roughly chopped

1 red pepper, roughly chopped

2 tbsp tomato puree

2 tsp Turkish pepper flakes

2 tsp dried thyme

1 tsp smoked paprika

1kg chicken thighs, skin on and bone in

400g boccole pasta

750ml hot chicken stock – from 1 stock cube

80g cream cheese

salt and pepper

You really can't beat a chicken–pasta combo – it's a classic that never gets old. This creamy traybake version is particularly delicious and rather easy to make. You start by blitzing a load of veggies into a sauce and slap that over some chicken. Pop it into the oven to roast and then clatter in some pasta to soak up all the yummy juices as it cooks right there in the roasting tin. I love using boccole pasta, a chubby tube, slightly shorter than penne. Don't worry if you can't find it; any small pasta shapes like shells or macaroni will work beautifully.

SERVES 4

1
Preheat the oven to 200°C/180°C fan/gas 6. Chuck the tomatoes, garlic cloves, onion, pepper, tomato puree, Turkish pepper flakes, thyme, smoked paprika and plenty of salt and pepper into a food processor and blitz until smooth.

2
Pop the chicken into a 30x40cm roasting tin and season with plenty of salt and pepper. Pour over the sauce and mix well. Arrange the chicken skin side up, cover with foil and roast in the oven for 30 minutes.

3
Tip the pasta into the tray around the chicken and pour in the stock. Stir together so the pasta is submerged and return to the oven and roast for 30 to 35 minutes or until the chicken is cooked and the pasta al dente.

4
Remove the chicken from the roasting tin and set to one side. Add the cream cheese to the pasta and mix well. If you have a thing for crispy chicken, feel free to grill it while you finish the pasta so it gets really golden all over. Whatever you decide, serve the chicken and creamy pasta immediately.

PREP:
12 minutes

COOK:
1 hour 5 minutes

PERSIAN-STYLE SAFFRON CHICKEN RICE

a pinch of saffron

2 tbsp just-boiled water

4 cloves of garlic, peeled and crushed

3 tbsp tomato puree

2 tbsp olive oil

juice of 1 orange

2 tsp ground coriander

½ tsp turmeric

¼ tsp ground cinnamon

500ml hot chicken stock – from 1 stock cube

1kg chicken thighs, skin on and bone in

250g basmati rice

3 cardamom pods, bashed open

a handful of barberries or pomegranate seeds

10g pistachios, roughly chopped

a handful of coriander leaves

300g Greek yoghurt – I use 10% fat

salt and pepper

Perfumed with saffron and cardamom, with crispy chicken and fluffy rice, this is one of the most exquisite traybakes around. I was inspired by a stunning Persian dish, *zereshk polo ba morgh*, or saffron-roasted chicken with rice and barberries. The OG recipe is all cooked separately, the chicken in one pot, crispy rice (this is known as a *tahdig*) in another and barberries candied in sugar syrup in another. Mine has more of a laid-back throw-it-all-in-the-oven vibe to get those crispy edges of golden rice and succulent juicy chicken thighs. I love piling on the garnishes for colour and texture – more is more in my opinion, but feel free to scale back if I've gone a little overboard.

SERVES 4

1
Preheat the oven to 200°C/180°C fan/gas 6. Put the saffron into a mixing bowl and add the just-boiled water. Stir and leave to infuse for a few minutes.

2
Add the garlic, tomato puree, olive oil, orange juice, coriander, turmeric, cinnamon and a very generous pinch of salt and pepper to the bowl with the saffron and mix it all into a paste.

3
Transfer half the saffron paste to the stock and whisk together. Tip the remaining saffron paste into a large mixing bowl, add the chicken and toss together.

4
Tip the rice into a 30x40cm roasting tin and pour over the stock. Add the cardamom pods and arrange the chicken over the top. Cover the tray with foil and bake for 30 minutes. Remove the foil and return to the oven for 20 to 25 minutes or until the chicken is golden and cooked through and the rice crispy on the top.

5
Garnish with the barberries or pomegranate seeds, pistachios and coriander leaves and serve immediately with yoghurt.

PREP:
10 minutes

COOK:
55 minutes

SPEEDY CHICKEN KORMA

- 1 onion, peeled and finely chopped
- 1 tbsp groundnut or neutral oil
- 600g boneless skinless chicken thigh fillets, cut into 1–2 cm strips
- 150g Greek yoghurt – I use 10% fat
- 4 cloves of garlic, peeled and crushed
- a 2–3cm piece of fresh ginger, peeled and grated
- 2 tsp garam masala
- ½ tsp turmeric
- ¼ tsp hot chilli powder
- 200ml just-boiled water
- 1 tbsp cashew butter
- 150ml double cream
- a handful of finely chopped coriander leaves
- salt and pepper

Made with subtle spices and a rich, creamy sauce infused with cashew nut butter, this quick-cook korma traybake is pure comfort food heaven. The cashew butter is a nod to the traditional North Indian kormas, which often use ground cashews or almonds (feel free to swap for almond butter if you prefer). As it melts into the sauce, it creates an indulgent, velvety texture that's hard to resist. For extra wow factor, you can load up on the garnishes, raining down toasted cashew nuts and fiery red chillies to contrast with that mellow yellow sauce.

SERVES 4

1
Preheat the oven to 220°C/200°C fan/gas 7. Chuck the onions into a 24x32cm roasting tin and add the oil and a pinch of salt and pepper. Roast in the oven for 10 minutes to get some colour on to the onions.

2
Put the chicken into a large mixing bowl and add the yoghurt, garlic, ginger, garam masala, turmeric, chilli powder and a big pinch of salt and pepper and mix well. Add to the roasting tin with the onions and pour in 200ml of just-boiled water. Stir together and put into the oven for 15 minutes to start cooking the chicken.

3
Remove the roasting tin from the oven, add the cashew butter and double cream and stir together. Return to the oven for 10 to 15 minutes or until the chicken is cooked through and the sauce all bubbling and thick. Give the korma a good stir and check the seasoning, adding salt to taste. Scatter over the coriander and serve immediately. I love this with fluffy basmati rice.

PREP:
10 minutes

COOK:
40 minutes

SUMAC-SPICED CHICKEN
WITH CARAMELIZED ONIONS

- 500g red onions, peeled and finely sliced
- 5 tbsp olive oil, plus extra for drizzling
- 1 tbsp + 2 tsp sumac
- 1 tsp caster sugar
- 150ml white wine or water
- 2 tbsp tomato puree
- 1 tbsp pomegranate molasses
- 1 tsp dried mint
- 4 cloves of garlic, peeled and crushed
- 4 chicken breasts (about 600g in total)
- 2 handfuls of parsley leaves
- juice of ½ a lemon
- salt and pepper

This super-juicy, sumac-spiced chicken and caramelized onion traybake is wholeheartedly inspired by one of my favourite Palestinian dishes, *musakhan*. The original is a much more elaborate affair, with bone-in chicken and onions slow cooked in generous amounts of olive oil and sumac for hours. I have borrowed a few elements to make this easy traybake, with succulent chicken breasts, which instantly feel healthy to me, sweet tangy onions and a lovely tart salad. It makes a luscious light supper, which you can bulk up for friends with a little yoghurt and some pillowy soft fresh pittas.

SERVES 4

1
Preheat the oven to 200°C/180°C fan/gas 6. Chuck the onions into a 24x32cm roasting tin. Add 3 tablespoons of the oil, 1 teaspoon of sumac, the sugar and plenty of salt and pepper and toss together. Pour in the wine or water. Scrunch up some baking paper and wet it under the cold tap. Spread it over the onions, tucking in the sides, and roast for 30 minutes so the onions start to caramelize.

2
Meanwhile, put the tomato puree, pomegranate molasses, 1 tablespoon of sumac, the dried mint, garlic, the remaining 2 tablespoons of olive oil and a good pinch of salt and pepper into a mixing bowl. Mix well, then add the chicken and mix again so it gets completely coated.

3
Remove the onions from the oven. Give them a good mix and place the chicken on top. Cover again with the baking paper and return to the oven for 30 to 35 minutes or until the chicken is cooked through and juicy.

4
Mix the parsley with the lemon juice, the remaining 1 teaspoon of sumac and a little drizzle of olive oil. Serve immediately with the chicken.

PREP:
15 minutes

COOK:
1 hour 5 minutes

CHEESY CHICKEN MELTS

4 chicken breasts
200g cream cheese
120g grated mozzarella (from a bag or the firm stuff)
1 clove of garlic, peeled and crushed
2 tbsp rose harissa
12 rashers of streaky bacon
salt

With a snap of your fingers and a little kitchen magic, transform a functional chicken breast into a lip-smackingly good, showstopping dinner with this harissa and mozzarella-stuffed chicken traybake. Simply bash out the chicken and stuff it with a cheesy mixture that pairs perfectly with the smoky kick of harissa, creating a flavour bomb of a filling that takes every bite to the next level. To seal the deal, wrap it tightly in rashers of streaky bacon. These crisp up to make it even more mouthwatering. Ideal for a week-night treat or a special occasion.

SERVES 4

1
Preheat the oven to 200°C/180°C fan/gas 6. Get two large pieces of baking paper and place one on a chopping board. Pop one of the chicken breasts on to it and cover with the other piece of baking paper. Get something solid, like a rolling pin, and bash the chicken until it's nice and thin, about half a centimetre. Repeat with the rest.

2
Mix the cream cheese, mozzarella, garlic, rose harissa and plenty of salt in a bowl.

3
Dollop a quarter of the mix in the middle of each piece of chicken, then make a parcel by folding the sides up tightly around the filling. Wrap each piece with bacon to hold everything together.

4
Put the chicken into a 30x40cm non-stick or lined roasting tin and roast for 20 to 25 minutes or until the chicken is cooked through and the bacon a little crispy. Serve immediately. It's fantastic with mash and your choice of salad.

PREP:
20 minutes

COOK:
25 minutes

BAHARAT-SPICED CHICKEN
AND SWEET POTATO WEDGES

900g sweet potatoes, cut into wedges – the big ones into 8 wedges and smaller ones into 6

2 tbsp olive oil

4 tbsp mayonnaise

2 tbsp tomato puree

2 tsp baharat

1 tsp smoked paprika

juice of ½ a lemon

3 cloves of garlic, peeled and crushed

1kg chicken thighs, skin on and bone in

a small handful of finely chopped parsley leaves

salt and pepper

If you're in the market for a comforting, no-fuss dinner, one that's so simple it feels like lazy cooking, then this sumptuous traybake is for you. What makes this really stand out is using a little mayonnaise in the marinade. Think of it a little like Meghan Markle – they are both huggers. The mayo cosies up around the meat, locking in the flavour of the spices and stopping them from burning. The sweet potatoes soak up all the luscious juices from the chicken, turning melt-in-your-mouth tender in the middle and a little crispy around the edges.

SERVES 4

1
Preheat the oven to 220ºC/200ºC fan/gas 7. Chuck the sweet potato wedges into a 30x40cm roasting tin and add the olive oil and plenty of salt and pepper. Toss together and roast for 20 minutes.

2
Meanwhile, pop the mayonnaise, tomato puree, baharat, smoked paprika, lemon juice, garlic and a good pinch of salt and pepper into a large mixing bowl and mix into a smooth paste. Add the chicken, mix well and leave to marinate while the potatoes cook.

3
Get the sweet potatoes out of the oven and reduce the temperature to 200ºC/180ºC fan/gas 6. Place the chicken skin side up on top of the sweet potatoes. Tip 150ml of water into the bowl the chicken was marinating in, swirl it round and pour into the roasting tin. Return to the oven for 40 to 45 minutes or until the chicken is cooked through and tender. Season to taste and scatter over the parsley before serving immediately.

PREP:
10 minutes

COOK:
1 hour 5 minutes

SWEET CHILLI AND TURMERIC ROASTED SALMON	102
PORK TENDERLOIN WITH CREAMY DIANE SAUCE	104
SEARED TUNA WITH BRAISED LENTILS AND GREEN OLIVE SALSA	106
BROWNED BUTTER DUKKAH PUMPKIN WITH HERBY HUMMUS	108
SPICED BEEF KOFTA AND CHARRED SMOKY VEG	110
LAMB CUTLETS WITH CRISPY POTATOES AND HALLOUMI IN A SALSA VERDE	112
HASSELBACK SQUASH WITH PRESERVED LEMON GREMOLATA	114
CRISPY SEABASS WITH ZINGY MINT SALSA	116
MEDITERRANEAN ROASTED PORK CHOPS WITH ZA'ATAR CROUTONS	118
KERALAN-STYLE MONKFISH CURRY	120
COURGETTE UPSIDE-DOWN TART	122
THE ULTIMATE TURKISH MEATBALL TRAYBAKE	124
STICKY GOCHUJANG AUBERGINES	126
MEDITERRANEAN COD WITH HERBY PARMESAN CRUMBLE	128

SWANKY RECIPES

By definition, 'swanky' means stylish and luxurious, and that's exactly the essence of this chapter. It's home to the kind of recipes you want in your back pocket when you need to pull out all the stops and impress. I've chosen premium cuts of meat and fish to bring a serious wow factor to your table, yet these dishes remain surprisingly approachable. They may look and taste like something from a swanky restaurant, but they're easy enough to recreate in your own kitchen.

SWEET CHILLI AND TURMERIC ROASTED SALMON

This mouthwatering roasted salmon traybake is inspired by a showstopping Vietnamese dish called *chả cá lã vọng*, a feast of golden spiced fish, served in a pan with loads of dill, spring onions and peanuts. In place of the fried fish, I use salmon, which I love to roast as the slightly fatty flesh stays really juicy and it will drink up anything it's paired with – in this case, a punchy marinade of turmeric, garlic, ginger and sweet chilli sauce. Toss in some rice noodles to soak up all the juices from the roasting tin, and for an extra pop of flavour, serve with a tangy dipping sauce.

for the marinade:
- 4 cloves of garlic, peeled and crushed
- 2 spring onions, finely chopped
- a 2–3cm piece of fresh ginger, peeled and grated
- ½ a red chilli, deseeded if you like and finely chopped
- juice of 1 lime, plus wedges to serve
- 2 tbsp fish sauce
- 2 tbsp sweet chilli sauce
- 1 tbsp groundnut or neutral oil
- 1 tsp turmeric

for the salmon:
- an 800g side of salmon, skin on
- 8 spring onions, roughly chopped into 3–5cm pieces
- 2 large handfuls of roughly chopped dill, plus another small handful, finely chopped
- 1 tbsp of groundnut or neutral oil
- 200g vermicelli rice noodles
- 30g roasted peanuts, roughly chopped
- ½ a red chilli, deseeded if you like and finely chopped

for the dipping sauce:
- 2 tbsp fish sauce
- 2 tbsp sweet chilli sauce
- juice of 1 lime

PREP: 20 minutes
COOK: 35 minutes
MARINATE: 10 minutes

SERVES 4

1
Preheat the oven to 200ºC/180ºC fan/gas 6. Mix all the ingredients for the marinade together. Put the salmon, skin side down, into a snug dish and pour the sauce over the top. Rub it all over and leave to marinate for 10 minutes.

2
Put the spring onions and the roughly chopped dill into a 24x32cm roasting tin. Add the oil and toss together. Place the salmon on top skin side down. Scoop out all the sauce from the marinating dish and pour over the fish. Add 4 tablespoons of water around the salmon and roast for 25 to 30 minutes or until the salmon is just cooked through.

3
Meanwhile, pop the noodles into a bowl and cover with just-boiled water. Give them a good mix so they are fully submerged and leave them for 4 to 5 minutes or until al dente. Drain and immerse in cold water to cool completely, then drain again.

4
Remove the salmon from the roasting tin and transfer to a plate. Cover with foil to keep warm. Chuck the noodles into the roasting tin and mix into all the juicy herbs. Return the tin to the oven for 5 minutes to warm through.

5
Mix the ingredients for the dipping sauce together with 4 tablespoons of water in a little serving bowl.

6
To serve, divide the noodles between 4 serving plates. Top with a piece of the salmon and garnish with the peanuts, chilli and the remaining dill. Serve immediately with lime wedges and the dipping sauce on the table.

PORK TENDERLOIN
WITH CREAMY DIANE SAUCE

500g closed-cup white mushrooms, finely sliced
2 tbsp olive oil
2 sprigs of thyme, leaves picked, or 1 tsp dried
600g pork tenderloin
1 tbsp + 1 tsp Dijon mustard
4–6 slices of Parma ham
300ml double cream
2 cloves of garlic, peeled and grated
2 tsp Worcester sauce
salt and pepper

If you're not familiar with the delights of a Diane sauce, let me shine a spotlight on her for you. She's a creamy retro-classic made from fried mushrooms cooked in juices of a pan-fried steak, often whipped up table-side for a little theatre in the heyday of swanky dining back in the 1930s. Instead of the classic pan-fried steak, I have used traybake-friendly pork tenderloin, wrapped in a snug layer of Parma ham to lock in those luscious juices. To complete your feast, I suggest buttery mash and a pile of simple green beans.

SERVES 4

1
Preheat the oven to 220°C/200°C fan/gas 7. Chuck the mushrooms into a 24x32cm roasting tin. Add the olive oil, thyme and a generous pinch of salt and pepper. Toss together and roast for 15 minutes to get some heat into the mushrooms.

2
Meanwhile, pat the pork dry and remove any sinew. Rub 1 tablespoon of the Dijon mustard all over and season heavily with salt and pepper. Cut the pork into two pieces and wrap each piece in 2 or 3 slices of the Parma ham, depending on the size of your ham.

3
Give the mushrooms a good mix and pop the two pieces of pork into the middle of the roasting tin. Return to the oven for 25 minutes or until the pork is just cooked through and the Parma ham crispy. Remove the pork from the roasting tin, cover and set to one side to rest.

4
Pour the cream into the roasting tin with the mushrooms and add the garlic, Worcester sauce, the remaining 1 teaspoon of mustard and a pinch of salt and pepper. Mix well and return to the oven for 5 to 6 minutes until the sauce is bubbling and rich.

5
Slice up the pork and pour all the resting juices into the sauce. Mix well and serve all together at the table.

PREP:
15 minutes

COOK:
46 minutes

SEARED TUNA
WITH BRAISED LENTILS AND GREEN OLIVE SALSA

for the tuna:
- 1 onion, peeled and finely chopped
- 2 cloves of garlic, peeled and finely chopped
- 2 x 400g tins of puy lentils, drained and rinsed
- 3 tbsp tomato puree
- 1 tsp dried thyme
- 200ml white wine
- 300ml hot chicken stock – from 1 stock cube
- 2 tbsp olive oil
- 500g loin of tuna, cut in half widthways
- salt and pepper

for the green olive salsa:
- a large handful of parsley leaves
- a large handful of mint leaves
- a large handful of tarragon leaves
- 100g pitted green olives
- 30g capers
- 8 anchovy fillets in oil, drained
- 4 tbsp olive oil
- 3 tsp Dijon mustard
- 2 cloves of garlic, peeled
- juice of 1 lemon

This traybake delivers a restaurant-quality meal with minimal effort, perfect for an elegant yet easy dinner. I use loin, but tuna steaks work just as well – adjust their cooking time, giving them a minute or two in the oven to finish. The fish is seared off until golden, then nestled into a roasting tin filled with a hearty puy lentil stew, simmered with plenty of onion, garlic, white wine and herbs. A tangy green olive salsa brings this rustic dish to life with a real sucker punch of tart flavours.

SERVES 4

1
Preheat the oven to 220ºC/200ºC fan/gas 7. Chuck the onion, garlic, lentils, tomato puree, thyme, white wine, stock and a good pinch of salt and pepper into a 24x32cm roasting tin. Cover with foil and pop into the oven for 1 hour until the lentils have absorbed most of the liquid and the onion is soft.

2
Meanwhile, make the green olive salsa by blending all the ingredients together with plenty of salt and pepper to taste. Give it a really good blast so it's lovely and fine.

3
Just before the lentils are ready, heat the olive oil in a frying pan over a high heat. Season the tuna with plenty of salt and sear in the pan for 2 to 3 minutes, turning every 30 to 40 seconds until the fish is a little golden all over. Transfer to the tray with the lentils, cover again with foil and return to the oven for 8 to 10 minutes or until the tuna is just cooked but still pink in the middle.

4
To serve, divide the lentils between four plates. Slice up the tuna and top each plate with a portion. Spoon over the salsa and serve immediately.

PREP:
10 minutes

COOK:
1 hour 10 minutes

BROWNED BUTTER DUKKAH PUMPKIN
WITH HERBY HUMMUS

If you're looking to impress any vegetarian friends or just embracing a more plant-based diet, this recipe is an absolute banger. The pumpkin is the star of the show, roasted to perfection until it's nutty, sweet and golden. It's then paired with a vibrant herby hummus and finished with a luxurious drizzle of dukkah butter. I love serving this alongside a tart green salad and warm flatbreads to complete the meal. No pumpkin? No problem. Just swap it for squash and you'll still get the same delicious vibes.

SERVES 4

for the pumpkin:
1kg peeled pumpkin, cut into 1cm slices
2 tbsp olive oil
50g butter
1½ tbsp dukkah
1 tsp Turkish pepper flakes
salt and pepper

for the herby hummus:
1 x 400g tin of chickpeas
juice of ½ a lemon
2 cloves of garlic, peeled
120g tahini
a large handful of coriander leaves
a large handful of parsley leaves, plus a few extra, finely chopped, to garnish
sea salt

1
Preheat the oven to 220°C/200°C fan/gas 7. Chuck the pumpkin slices into a 30x40cm roasting tin, add the olive oil and a good pinch of salt and pepper and toss together. Roast for 35 to 40 minutes or until tender and a little golden.

2
Meanwhile, make the herby hummus. Drain the chickpeas, reserving the liquid from the tin, and blitz them in a blender with 120ml of the chickpea water, the lemon juice, garlic cloves, tahini, coriander and parsley leaves and a good pinch of sea salt until smooth and creamy.

3
Melt the butter in a small saucepan over a medium heat. Add the dukkah and a pinch of salt. Swirl around and cook, stirring occasionally, for 2 to 3 minutes until the butter browns and goes nutty. You can spoon off the foam if you're feeling swanky.

4
To serve, swirl the hummus on to a serving plate. Top it with the pumpkin slices and spoon over the dukkah butter. Garnish with a little finely chopped parsley and the Turkish pepper flakes.

PREP:
20 minutes

COOK:
40 minutes

SPICED BEEF KOFTA
AND CHARRED SMOKY VEG

for the vegetables:
2 aubergines
4 tomatoes
2 red peppers
1 bulb of garlic, left whole
2 tbsp olive oil
juice of ½ a lemon
salt and pepper

for the kofta:
1 onion, peeled
600g minced beef – I use 20% fat
4 cloves of garlic, peeled and grated
2 tsp Turkish pepper flakes
1 tsp paprika
½ tsp ground black pepper
a handful of roughly chopped parsley leaves
4 flatbreads

PREP:
25 minutes

COOK:
1 hour 30 minutes

When you think of cooking a kebab, it's almost impossible not to imagine the sizzle of meat hitting a grill and the tantalizing aroma of spices. Although less dramatic, there are equally delicious oven-ready kebabs found across the Middle East that skip the grill but never skimp on flavour. This is my version. Beautifully spiced minced-beef kofta are cooked over a medley of roasted vegetables that soak up all those rich, savoury juices. Some traditional recipes take it up a notch, encasing the whole dish in a thin, crisp layer of dough and serving it alongside creamy yoghurt, a parsley and red onion salad and heaps of warm bread. Whipping up any kind of quick dough is my idea of hell, so I leave that bit out, but I am all in for the sides.

SERVES 4

1
Preheat the oven to 220°C/200°C fan/gas 7. Prick a few holes through the skin of the aubergines and chuck them into a 30x40xm roasting tin. Add the tomatoes and peppers.

2
Wrap the garlic bulb in foil and pop that into the roasting tin with the vegetables. Pop that lot into the oven for 1 hour to 1 hour 20 minutes or until everything is soft and squidgy. Remove the vegetables from the roasting tin and transfer to a mixing bowl to cool slightly.

3
While the vegetables are cooking, prepare the kofta kebabs. Grate the onion into a little bowl, using the coarse side of a cheese grater. Use your hands to squeeze out the excess moisture, then chuck the onion into a large mixing bowl and add the beef, grated garlic, Turkish pepper flakes, paprika, black pepper and a large pinch of salt. Mix it all together really well. Divide into 8 portions and roll each out into an 8cm-ish sausage shape. Put them on a plate and pop them into the fridge until needed.

4
Once cool enough to peel, remove the skin from the aubergines, tomatoes and peppers and finely chop into a salsa situation. Return to the roasting tin. Unwrap the garlic, squish the cloves out of their skins, mash and add to the roasting tin with the vegetables. Add the olive oil, lemon juice and a good pinch of salt and pepper. Mix well and spread out into an even layer.

5
Place the kebabs on top of the vegetables and return to the oven for 8 to 10 minutes or until the kebabs are just cooked through. Scatter over the parsley and serve immediately with the flatbreads.

LAMB CUTLETS
WITH CRISPY POTATOES AND HALLOUMI IN A SALSA VERDE

for the lamb:

850g baking potatoes, cut into 1–2cm cubes

2½ tbsp olive oil

250g block of halloumi, cut into 1–2cm cubes

8 lamb cutlets (about 800g in total), at room temperature

150g frozen peas

salt and pepper

for the salsa verde:

4 tbsp olive oil

juice of 1 lemon

4–6 anchovy fillets in oil (I use 6)

2 cloves of garlic, peeled

2 large handfuls of parsley leaves

1 large handful of basil leaves

1 tbsp drained capers

PREP:
15 minutes

COOK:
50 minutes

Lamb, halloumi and potatoes are a match made in culinary heaven, and when combined, they always deliver something exceptional. This elevated traybake brings these three together with a zingy salsa verde that perfectly balances the richness of the lamb. To make each ingredient shine, cook them at different stages: this way you get crispy potatoes, charred cubes of halloumi and tender pink lamb.

SERVES 4

1
Preheat the oven to 220°C/200°C fan/gas 7. Chuck the potatoes into a 30x40cm non-stick or lined roasting tin. Add 1 tablespoon of olive oil and plenty of salt and pepper. Toss together and roast for 30 minutes until the potatoes are starting to get crispy.

2
Meanwhile, make the salsa verde by blitzing everything together with a good pinch of salt and pepper and 2 tablespoons of water using a mini chopper until you have a smooth-ish salsa. If you want more texture you can stir in some extra capers before serving.

3
Pop the halloumi into a bowl and add half a tablespoon of olive oil. Mix well and add to the potatoes. Return to the oven and cook for 10 minutes until the halloumi is a little golden at the edges.

4
Rub half a tablespoon of olive oil over the lamb chops and season both sides with salt and pepper.

5
Scatter the peas into the tray with the potatoes and place the lamb on top. Return to the oven for 5 minutes to get some heat into the lamb.

6
While the lamb cooks, preheat the last half a tablespoon of oil in a non-stick pan over a high heat. Add the chops and sear them for 30 seconds – 1 minute a side until a little golden but still pink in the middle.

7
To serve, divide the potatoes, halloumi and peas between four plates. Top each with two chops and drizzle plenty of salsa verde over the top.

HASSELBACK SQUASH
WITH PRESERVED LEMON GREMOLATA

for the squash:
1 butternut squash
1 tbsp olive oil
10g toasted pine nuts
salt and pepper

for the butter:
40g butter, at room temperature
80g sun-dried tomatoes in oil, drained and finely chopped
2 cloves of garlic, peeled and crushed

for the preserved lemon gremolata:
3 tbsp olive oil
1 preserved lemon, seeds removed
1 green chilli, deseeded if you like
1 clove of garlic, peeled
2 handfuls of parsley leaves
1 handful of coriander leaves
juice of 1 lemon

for the tahini sauce:
120g tahini
120ml water
1 clove of garlic, peeled and crushed
juice of ½ a lemon

PREP:
25 minutes

COOK:
50 minutes

This is the ultimate vegetarian showstopper, easily made vegan with a simple swap to vegan butter. It takes the humble butternut squash and transforms it into something truly spectacular. The squash is hasselbacked – sliced into delicate accordion-like slits, which absorb every drop of the umami-rich sun-dried-tomato butter.

SERVES 4

1
Preheat the oven to 200°C/180°C fan/gas 6. To prep the squash, top and tail it and peel off the skin with a peeler, then cut it in half lengthways and scoop out the seeds. Lay one half, cut side down, on to a chopping board and place two wooden chopsticks either side. You want to cut slits every half centimetre into the squash, using the chopsticks as a buffer so you don't cut all the way though. Repeat with the other half.

2
Pop the squash halves into a 24x32cm roasting tin, cut side down still, and pour over the oil. Season with a load of salt and pepper and roast for 40 to 45 minutes until the fattest part is tender.

3
Meanwhile, mix the butter together with the sundried tomatoes, garlic and a little pinch of salt and pepper. You can blitz them together in a mini chopper to save time.

4
Then make the gremolata by blitzing everything together in a mini chopper with a pinch of salt and pepper until you have a lovely fine salsa.

5
Finally make the tahini sauce, whisking everything together with a pinch of salt until smooth and creamy.

6
Take the squash out of the oven and spread the butter over the top, making sure it squidges into the gaps. Return to the oven for 5 minutes until the butter has completely melted.

7
To serve, pour the tahini sauce on to a serving platter. Add the squash and spoon over any butter from the roasting tin. Drizzle over the preserved lemon gremolata and scatter over the pine nuts. Serve immediately.

CRISPY SEABASS
WITH ZINGY MINT SALSA

for the seabass:
850g courgettes, cut into 1cm cubes
4 tbsp olive oil
1 x 400g tin of chickpeas, drained and rinsed
juice of ½ a lemon
4 seabass fillets (400–500g in total)
30g unsalted shelled pistachios, roughly chopped
salt and pepper

for the salsa:
a large handful of finely chopped mint leaves
3 tbsp olive oil
1 tbsp white wine vinegar
juice of ½ a lemon
1 clove of garlic, peeled and crushed
1 tsp sumac
1 tsp Turkish pepper flakes, plus extra to serve

This dish brings swanky restaurant vibes straight to your gorgeous kitchen in the simplest of traybakes. How good is that? Think crispy seabass fillets roasted to perfection alongside golden, caramelized courgettes and irresistibly crispy chickpeas. That's topped off with a tangy mint and sumac salsa that cuts through the richness of the fish beautifully. It's downright elegant and screaming out for a glass of chilled vino.

SERVES 4

1
Preheat the oven to 220°C/200°C fan/gas 7. Chuck the courgettes into a 30x40cm non-stick or lined roasting tin. Add 2 tablespoons of the olive oil and plenty of salt and pepper. Toss together and roast for 25 minutes until starting to go golden.

2
Meanwhile, pat the chickpeas dry with kitchen paper, pop them into a mixing bowl and add 1 tablespoon of the oil, the lemon juice and a pinch of salt. Toss together and add to the courgettes. Mix well and return to the oven to roast for 30 to 35 minutes, mixing halfway until everything is golden and a little crispy.

3
To make the salsa, put all the ingredients into a bowl with a pinch of salt. Mix well and set to one side.

4
Just before the courgettes and chickpeas are done, heat the remaining 1 tablespoon of oil in a non-stick frying pan over a high heat. Pat the seabass dry and season both sides with salt. Cook in two batches, placing the fish into the pan, skin side down. Sear for 1 to 1½ minutes until the skin is golden. Press the fillets down with a spatula to stop them curling. Place the fish on to the courgettes and return to the oven for 3 to 5 minutes or until the seabass is just cooked through.

5
To serve, divide the courgettes and chickpeas between four serving plates. Top each with a seabass fillet and spoon over the dressing. Scatter over the pistachio nuts and some extra Turkish pepper flakes.

PREP:
20 minutes

COOK:
1 hour 5 minutes

This restaurant-worthy feast feels like something you'd find at your favourite local joint. Juicy charred pork chops sit on a base of crispy za'atar croutons and tender roasted vegetables, doused in a garlicky lemon dressing.

MEDITERRANEAN ROASTED PORK CHOPS
WITH ZA'ATAR CROUTONS

SERVES 2

for the traybake:
- 1 red onion, peeled and cut into 2cm pieces
- 1 red pepper, cut into 2–3cm pieces
- 1 courgette, cut into 2–3cm pieces
- 1 aubergine, cut into 2–3cm pieces
- 100g white bread without crusts
- 2 tbsp olive oil
- 1 tbsp za'atar
- 1 tbsp groundnut or neutral oil
- 2 thick-cut pork chops (about 250g each), at room temperature
- 60g feta
- salt and pepper

for the dressing:
- 3 tbsp olive oil
- juice of 1 lemon
- 2 tsp Dijon mustard
- 1 clove of garlic, peeled and crushed
- 2 tsp dried oregano
- ½ tsp chilli flakes

PREP:
15 minutes

COOK:
40 minutes

1
Preheat the oven to 220ºC/200ºC fan/gas 7. Start with the dressing. Whisk together the olive oil, lemon juice, mustard, garlic, oregano, chilli flakes and plenty of salt and pepper.

2
For the traybake, pop the red onion, pepper, courgette and aubergine pieces into a 30x40cm roasting tin. Add two-thirds of the dressing and toss together. Roast for 20 minutes to start cooking the vegetables.

3
Meanwhile, rip the bread into 2–3cm pieces and put into a mixing bowl. Add the olive oil, za'atar and a pinch of salt. Toss it all together and add to the roasting tin with the veg. Return the tin to the oven for 10 minutes so the bread can start to crisp up.

4
While that cooks, preheat the groundnut or neutral oil in a non-stick frying pan over a high heat. Season the pork chops with plenty of salt and pepper. Sear them for 3 to 4 minutes on each side until golden.

5
Take the roasting tin out of the oven and reduce the heat to 200ºC/180ºC fan/gas 6. Give the veg a mix and make space for the pork in the middle. Add the chops and return to the oven for 8 to 10 minutes or until the pork is just cooked through and the croutons are really crispy.

6
Pop the pork to one side to rest for 5 minutes and divide the veg and those insanely crunchy croutons between two serving bowls. Drizzle over the remaining dressing and rip over the feta in big chunks.

7
Add the pork to the serving bowls and season the resting juices with salt and pepper to taste. Spoon them all over the top, grab your cutlery and dive on in.

KERALAN-STYLE MONKFISH CURRY

This traybake is my love letter to one of the most beautiful places in the world: Kerala, in southern India. Lush and green, and blessed with a cool coastal cuisine that I just adore. I'm bringing some of those bold flavours – think tamarind, coconut and curry leaves – together to create a fragrant sauce for monkfish. Now, monkfish is expensive, so please treat it well. It hates to be overcooked, and if you can, make sure you pair it with fresh curry leaves, so it gets the full flavour effect from them. As for tamarind, its tangy, sour kick can vary between brands, so give it a taste first to gauge its intensity before adding.

SERVES 4

- 1 onion, peeled and roughly chopped
- 300g cherry tomatoes, halved
- 4 tbsp groundnut or neutral oil
- 1 x 400g tin of coconut milk
- 1 tbsp tamarind paste
- 4 cloves of garlic, peeled and crushed
- a 2–3cm piece of fresh ginger, peeled and grated
- 1 tsp garam masala
- 500g monkfish, cut into 2–3cm pieces
- 200g raw peeled king prawns
- 2 tsp mild-medium chilli powder
- 1 tsp turmeric
- 2 tsp black mustard seeds
- a large handful of fresh curry leaves
- salt

1
Preheat the oven to 220°C/200°C fan/gas 7. Chuck the chopped onion and tomatoes into a 24x32cm roasting tin and add 1 tablespoon of the oil and a pinch of salt. Toss together and pop into the oven for 10 minutes to soften everything.

2
Meanwhile, whisk together the coconut milk, tamarind, garlic, ginger, garam masala and a pinch of salt. Pour into the roasting tin with the onions and tomatoes and return to the oven for 8 to 10 minutes or until bubbling.

3
Put the monkfish and prawns into a mixing bowl, add the chilli powder, turmeric and a pinch of salt and mix together. Then – I know it's annoying – take out the prawns and set them to one side. Add the monkfish to the roasting tin, stir into the sauce and put into the oven so the fish can start cooking. After 5 minutes, add the prawns, stir together and return to the oven for a further 4 to 5 minutes or until the fish is cooked and the prawns all coral pink.

4
While the fish cooks, make a flavoured oil, or *tadka*, by heating the remaining 3 tablespoons of oil in a small non-stick frying pan. Add the black mustard seeds and curry leaves. Let them crackle in the oil for about a minute until the leaves go crispy. Spoon the fragrant oil and all the spices over the curry and mix well. Check the seasoning, adding salt to taste and more tamarind if needed, and serve immediately. I love this with loads of plain rice.

PREP:
15 minutes

COOK:
30 minutes

COURGETTE UPSIDE-DOWN TART

SERVES 4

500g courgettes, cut into 0.5cm rounds
1 tbsp olive oil
250g mascarpone
2 tsp Turkish pepper flakes
2 tsp sumac
1 tsp dried mint
320g packet of puff pastry – I use Jus-Rol
150g halloumi, coarsely grated
80g rocket
juice of ½ a lemon
salt and pepper

PREP:
12 minutes

COOK:
1 hour 5 minutes

This upside-down pastry tart uses a killer combo of courgettes and halloumi for the filling, with a little spiced mascarpone to keep it indulgent. It's what swanky light lunches are made of.

1
Preheat the oven to 220°C/200°C fan/gas 7 and line a 30x40cm roasting tin. Pop the courgettes into a mixing bowl and add the olive oil and plenty of salt and pepper. Mix well. Transfer to the roasting tin and arrange in an even layer on the bottom. Roast for 30 to 35 minutes in the oven or until the courgettes are golden on the bottom.

2
Meanwhile, mix the mascarpone together with the Turkish pepper flakes, sumac, mint and plenty of salt and pepper.

3
Unroll the puff pastry on to a kitchen surface, keeping it on the non-stick paper it comes with. Don't worry if it cracks a little. Dollop the mascarpone over the top and gently spread it out, leaving a 1 cm gap around the edges. Don't push too hard when you spread, or the pasty will stick to the baking paper.

4
Take the courgettes out of the oven and push them towards the middle of the roasting tin, keeping them in an even layer, just a bit closer together so the pastry will fit over the top. Scatter over the halloumi.

5
Holding it by the baking paper, turn the puff pastry upside-down and lay it over the courgettes. Gently peel off the baking paper and carefully press the pastry down over the courgettes, pushing the sides down tightly. Poke a few holes across the top of the pastry to let the steam out and roast for 25 to 30 minutes in the oven or until the pastry is golden.

6
Remove from the oven and leave to cool for 5 minutes in the roasting tin (it will de-puff as it cools). Get a chopping board that covers the roasting tin and very carefully – use oven gloves please – flip the tart out of the tin and on to the chopping board. Remove the baking paper liner and leave to cool for another 5 to 10 minutes so the pastry can firm up a little.

7
While you're waiting, dress the rocket with the lemon juice and a pinch of salt. Scatter over the top of the tart and serve immediately.

THE ULTIMATE TURKISH MEATBALL TRAYBAKE

for the vegetables:
1 large aubergine, cut into 5cm chunks
1 red onion, peeled and roughly chopped
2 red peppers, cut into 2–3cm pieces
300g cherry tomatoes
2 tbsp olive oil
2 tsp dried oregano
1 tsp Turkish pepper flakes
a small handful of roughly chopped parsley leaves
salt and pepper

for the meatballs:
1 onion, peeled
500g minced beef – I use 20% fat
2 tsp garlic powder
2 tsp Turkish pepper flakes
a handful of finely chopped parsley leaves
40g breadcrumbs
1 small free-range egg

for the tomato sauce:
2 tbsp tomato puree
2 tsp garlic powder
1 beef stock cube
150ml just-boiled water
450g tomato passata

This is my version of a classic Turkish traybake, where little meatballs are baked in a rich tomato sauce. Traditionally, this would all be cooked together with potatoes and veggies. This is proper hearty home cooking, and to be honest, I haven't messed with it much. I swap out the potatoes in favour of more veggies, and to keep the meatballs super juicy, I add them for the last few minutes of the cooking process along with the sauce.

SERVES 4

1
Preheat the oven to 220°C/200°C fan/gas 7. Pop the aubergine, onion, peppers and tomatoes into a 30x40cm roasting tin. Add the olive oil, oregano, Turkish pepper flakes and loads of salt and pepper. Toss together and roast for 30 to 35 minutes or until soft and a little golden.

2
Meanwhile make the meatballs. Grate the onion into a large mixing bowl and add the minced beef, garlic powder, Turkish pepper flakes, parsley, breadcrumbs, egg and loads of salt and pepper and mix together. Roll into 12 balls.

3
Whisk together the tomato puree, garlic powder, stock cube and 150ml of just-boiled water until smooth. Add the passata and mix. Check the seasoning, adding salt to taste.

4
Reduce the temperature to 200°C/180°C fan/gas 6. Nestle the meatballs into the veg and pour over the tomato sauce, making sure the meatballs are covered. Return to the oven and roast for 15 to 20 minutes or until the meatballs are just cooked through. Serve immediately with a little parsley scattered over the top.

PREP:
20 minutes

COOK:
1 hour

STICKY GOCHUJANG AUBERGINES

3 tbsp gochujang paste – I use a mild one made by Sun Hee
2 tbsp groundnut or neutral oil
2 tsp sesame oil
2 tsp light soy sauce
2 tsp caster sugar
4 cloves of garlic, peeled and grated
a 2–3cm piece of fresh ginger, peeled and grated
3 aubergines, cut into 5cm chunks (about 1kg in total)
2 tbsp dark soy sauce
4 spring onions, finely chopped
optional: 2 tsp toasted sesame seeds

You know those fancy South-east Asian restaurants – the ones with killer cocktails and small plates – where there's always an aubergine dish that steals the show? Dark, sticky and braised to perfection, it ends up being the highlight of the night. Well, this gochujang aubergine traybake is that dish. The aubergines soak up an umami-packed sauce that gets richer, stickier and more intense as they soften in the oven. Pair it with some sticky rice and, if you're feeling fancy, a mango martini on the side. Absolute heaven – just saying!

SERVES 4

1
Preheat the oven to 200°C/180°C fan/gas 6. Pop the gochujang, oil, sesame oil, light soy, sugar, garlic, ginger and 3 tablespoons of water into a mixing bowl. Whisk together until smooth. Chuck in the aubergines and toss together, then transfer to a 30x40cm roasting tin.

2
Pour 200ml of water into the mixing bowl you had the aubergines in and swirl it round, making sure to catch all the leftover marinade from the sides. Add the dark soy sauce, mix together to create a stock and pour into the roasting tin. Cover with foil and roast for 25 minutes to steam the aubergines a little. Remove the foil and give the tin a shake. Return to the oven for 25 to 30 minutes or until the aubergines are soft and sticky, giving them a stir halfway through.

3
Scatter over the spring onions and sesame seeds, if using, and serve immediately. I like this with plenty of jasmine rice.

PREP:
10 minutes

COOK:
55 minutes

This sophisticated seafood supper has the wow factor you want when you are looking to impress. Tender, flaky cod fillets are roasted with tomatoes and olives, beautiful fresh flavours that complement the fish rather than overpowering it. That's topped off with a herby green Parmesan crumble, which adds much needed crunch and a dollop of savoury goodness that melts though everything. The best bit, and perhaps don't highlight this to your esteemed guests: it's easy to prepare and cooks in under 15 minutes. Who says impressive can't be easy?

MEDITERRANEAN COD WITH HERBY PARMESAN CRUMBLE

SERVES 2

- 4 boneless skinless cod fillets (about 130g each)
- 240g cherry tomatoes, finely chopped
- 60g pitted Kalamata olives, finely chopped
- 2 cloves of garlic, peeled and finely chopped
- a large handful of finely chopped dill
- juice of 1 lemon
- 2 tbsp olive oil, plus extra for drizzling
- 2 tsp Turkish pepper flakes
- 100g stale bread, roughly chopped, or use breadcrumbs
- 100g Parmesan cheese, roughly chopped
- a large handful of parsley leaves
- salt and pepper

1
Preheat the oven to 200ºC/180ºC fan/gas 6. Season the fish and put into a 30x40cm non-stick or lined roasting tin.

2
Chuck the cherry tomatoes, olives, garlic, dill, lemon juice, olive oil, Turkish pepper flakes and a good pinch of salt and pepper into a bowl and mix together.

3
Pop the bread or breadcrumbs, Parmesan, parsley and a pinch of salt and pepper into a mini chopper and blend until fine.

4
Spoon the tomato mixture, and all the juices, over the top of the fish. Divide the Parmesan breadcrumbs over the top so each piece of fish gets a lovely mound of the crumble. Drizzle a little oil over the top and roast for 10 to 12 minutes or until the fish is just cooked and the top of the breadcrumbs is a little golden. Serve immediately. It pairs perfectly with buttery new potatoes and green beans.

PREP:
12 minutes

COOK:
12 minutes

MELTINGLY TENDER BEEF BRISKET RAGU	132
SAUSAGE CASSOULET WITH PARMESAN CRUMBLE	134
STUFFED AUBERGINES WITH JAMMY TOMATOES	136
DETROIT PIZZA	138
LOW AND SLOW HARISSA LAMB	140
SMOKY 'NDUJA BOSTON BEANS	142
KOREAN-STYLE BEEF SHORT RIBS	144
SLOW-COOKED PULLED PORK TACOS	146
MOROCCAN LAMB WITH COUSCOUS	148
VENISON CHILLI CON CARNE	150
CROATIAN-STYLE BEEF PAŠTICADA	152
LEBANESE-LANCASHIRE HOT POT	154
SLOW-COOKED COCONUT BEEF CURRY	156
GREEK-ISH LAMB STIFADO	158
STICKY SOY AND GINGER PORK BELLY	160
IRAQI-STYLE STUFFED ONIONS	162

SLOW RECIPES

This chapter is perfect for those times when you can take it slow and let something delicious simmer and roast for hours while you sit back and relax. Low-and-slow cooking works magic on tougher cuts of meat, transforming them into melt-in-your-mouth masterpieces. Best of all, the prep is often minimal, as the oven takes care of the hard work for you. You'll also find recipes here that are ideal for feeding a crowd, featuring larger cuts of meat that make entertaining effortless.

MELTINGLY TENDER BEEF BRISKET RAGU

- 1kg beef brisket
- 2 tsp garlic powder
- 2 tsp smoked paprika
- 1 onion, peeled and finely chopped
- 1 carrot, peeled and finely chopped
- 2 sticks of celery, finely chopped
- 3 sprigs of thyme
- 1 x 750ml bottle of red wine
- 2 x 400g tins of chopped tomatoes
- 2 tbsp sun-dried tomato puree
- 1 beef stock cube
- 200ml just-boiled water
- salt and pepper

Although this recipe takes its time in the oven, it's incredibly easy to put together. Simply toss the beef and everything for the sauce into a roasting tray and let the oven work its magic. Aside from the occasional check-in to top up the liquid, frankly, boiling the pasta takes more elbow grease than the ragu itself. Once the beef is super soft, shred it with two forks straight into the luscious tomato sauce. For a comforting meal, try serving with buttery tagliatelle, cheesy polenta or fluffy baked potatoes.

SERVES 6

1
Preheat the oven to 180°C/160°C fan/gas 4. Season the beef all over with the garlic powder, smoked paprika and plenty of salt and pepper.

2
Chuck the onion, carrot, celery, thyme, red wine, tomatoes and sun-dried tomato puree into a 24x32cm roasting tin. Crumble in the stock cube, stir it all together and add the beef. It should be 90% submerged. Scrunch up some baking paper and wet it under the cold tap. Spread this over the beef and tuck in the sides. Cover the whole tray with foil and roast for 3 hours.

3
Remove the beef from the oven and turn the brisket over. Add 100ml of just-boiled water. Cover again with the baking paper and foil and return to the oven for another hour. Check the beef. You should be able to pull it apart with a fork at its thickest point. If it's not ready, add another 100ml of just-boiled water to the sauce and return to the oven, all covered up, for another hour or until it's tender. Shred the beef completely and mix well into the sauce (fish out the thyme sprigs first). Check the seasoning, adding salt and pepper to taste, and serve immediately.

PREP:
15 minutes

COOK:
5 hours

SAUSAGE CASSOULET
WITH PARMESAN CRUMBLE

2 leeks, finely sliced

80g lardons or cubed bacon

2 tbsp olive oil

12 best quality pork sausages (800g in total)

300ml hot chicken stock – from 1 stock cube

200ml double cream

3 cloves of garlic, peeled and crushed

2 tsp Dijon mustard

1 tsp dried thyme

2 x 400g tins of cannellini beans, drained and rinsed

40g white breadcrumbs

20g Parmesan cheese, grated

salt and pepper

This is my kind of comfort food. A rich, creamy sausage casserole loaded with smoky bacon, tender leeks and velvety soft beans, all topped with an utterly irresistible Parmesan crumble. It screams cosy cooking after a long blustery walk, with a huge glass of red wine. To keep things super easy, I skip browning the sausages before popping them in the oven, but if you're in the mood, feel free to fry them lightly first, before assembling everything in the roasting tin.

SERVES 4

1
Preheat the oven to 220°C/200°C fan/gas 7. Chuck the leeks and lardons or bacon into a 24x32cm roasting tin and add the oil and plenty of salt and pepper. Mix together and roast for 20 minutes until the leeks look a little charred. Give them another good mix and add the sausages. Roast for another 10 minutes to start them cooking.

2
Meanwhile, whisk the stock together with the cream, garlic, mustard, thyme and a pinch of salt and pepper.

3
Take the roasting tin out of the oven and turn the temperature down to 200°C/180°C fan/gas 6. Pop the beans into the tin and pour over the creamy stock. Give everything a good mix, pushing the sausages into the beans so they are mostly covered by the sauce. Return to the oven for 40 to 45 minutes or until the top is golden and bubbling.

4
While this cooks, mix the breadcrumbs together with the Parmesan. Scatter evenly over the top of the cassoulet and return to the oven for 10 to 15 minutes until golden and crispy. Serve immediately.

PREP:
10 minutes

COOK:
1 hour 30 minutes

STUFFED AUBERGINES
WITH JAMMY TOMATOES

1 onion, peeled and finely sliced
4 small aubergines (about 250g each)
1kg tomatoes, roughly chopped
3 tbsp tomato puree
5 cloves of garlic, peeled and crushed
3 tsp Turkish pepper flakes
2 tsp sumac
1½ tsp dried mint
200ml just-boiled water
350g minced lamb – I use 20% fat
2 tbsp olive oil
200g Greek yoghurt – I use 10% fat
salt and pepper

PREP:
20 minutes

COOK:
1 hour 45 minutes

This Turkish-inspired traybake is bursting with flavour. Silky soft aubergines stuffed with spiced lamb mince, all nestled in a rich, garlicky tomato sauce with slow-cooked onions. Inspired by the traditional dish *karnıyarık* – which translates as 'split belly', in reference to the stuffed aubergines. Think of it as the meaty cousin of *ımam bayıldı*, perfect for anyone familiar with the beloved vegetarian version.

SERVES 4

1
Preheat the oven to 200°C/180°C fan/gas 6. Pop the onion into a 30x40cm roasting tin and add a pinch of salt and pepper.

2
Prick the aubergines with a knife to let out the steam and place them on top of the onions. Pack the tomatoes in all around them.

3
Mix together 2 tablespoons of tomato puree, 3 of the cloves of garlic, 2 teaspoons of Turkish pepper flakes, 1 teaspoon of sumac, 1 teaspoon of mint, the 200ml of just-boiled water and plenty of salt and pepper. Pour into the roasting tin and cover with foil. Roast for an hour to soften the aubergines, then remove the foil and return the tin to the oven for 30 minutes to get some colour on everything.

4
Meanwhile, chuck the lamb into a bowl and add the remaining 1 tablespoon of tomato puree, the remaining 2 cloves of garlic, 1 teaspoon of Turkish pepper flakes, 1 teaspoon of sumac, half a teaspoon of dried mint and a big pinch of salt and pepper. Mix well.

5
Remove the roasting tin from the oven. It will look a little dry, but don't worry, the lamb will make everything super juicy. Make a slit lengthways down the middle of each aubergine, pull them open – use two forks so you don't get burned – and spoon in the lamb mixture. Drizzle the olive oil over everything and return to the oven for 12 to 15 minutes or until the lamb is just cooked through. Serve immediately with loads of the jammy tomatoes on top and a big dollop of yoghurt.

DETROIT PIZZA

SERVES 2

for the dough:
210ml warm water
7g dried instant yeast
a big pinch of salt – I use 2 tsp sea salt here
300g strong white bread flour
olive oil, for greasing

for the sauce:
1 x 400g tin of chopped tomatoes
½ tsp garlic powder
½ tsp dried oregano
salt and pepper

for the toppings:
150g Cheddar cheese, grated
150g firm mozzarella, grated
18 slices of pepperoni (about 100g in total) or a vegetarian topping of your choice
Parmesan cheese (or a vegetarian alternative), grated, to serve

PREP:
12 minutes

COOK:
18 minutes

REST:
2 hours 20 minutes

I am so happy to welcome you to the wild world of Detroit pizza, a deep-dish rectangular traybake pizza that takes crispy, cheesy indulgence to the next level.

1
Pour the warm water into a large mixing bowl and add the yeast and salt. Whisk together until foamy and then add the flour. Mix to combine into a sticky dough. Cover and leave to rest for 10 minutes.

2
You're going to do an easy style of kneading called 'stretch and pull'. Stretch one end of the dough up and pull it over the rest. Repeat 10 times, working the gluten so the dough firms up a little. Transfer the dough into a large, oiled bowl and cover with cling film. Leave to rest for 2 hours in a warm dark place so it can double in size.

3
Meanwhile, prepare the sauce. Strain the tomatoes through a sieve for 5 minutes to remove the watery juices, then put the now-thick chopped tomatoes into a little saucepan. Add the garlic powder, oregano and loads of salt and pepper. Stir together and set to one side.

4
Preheat the oven to 250ºC/230ºC fan/gas 9. Rub a little oil all around a 24x32cm roasting tin. Transfer the dough to the roasting tin and spread it out over the bottom as best you can. Cover and leave for 10 minutes to soften, then go back to even it out. It will be much easier to work with now.

5
Scatter 60g of the Cheddar and 60g of the mozzarella over the pizza and put it into the oven to roast for 8 minutes. Remove from the oven and arrange the pepperoni (if using) over the top and then scatter over the remaining 90g of each cheese, making sure to get loads right into the edges of the roasting tin so they go super crispy. Return to the oven and cook for 8 to 10 minutes until the top is all bubbling and the sides are really golden. Remove from the oven and leave to cool for 5 minutes.

6
Meanwhile, gently heat the tomato sauce over a medium heat for a few minutes to warm through.

7
Separate the pizza from the roasting tin by running a knife between the pizza edge and roasting tin. Then get a spatula to loosen it underneath. Run it round the tray, loosening the pizza, so you can lift it out in one piece and on to a wooden board. Spoon two long lines of sauce down the length of the pizza, almost like car lanes. You most likely won't use all the sauce so save it for the next one or have it on the side for dipping. Rain down a load of Parmesan, slice and serve immediately.

LOW AND SLOW HARISSA LAMB

700g boneless leg of lamb, cut into 2–3cm pieces

1 tbsp ras el hanout

2 onions, peeled and roughly sliced

1 x 400g tin of chickpeas, drained and rinsed

500g tomato passata

2 tbsp rose harissa

2 tsp garlic powder

1 tsp smoked paprika

a handful of coriander leaves

salt and pepper

One of the many reasons I adore traybake cooking is its back-to-basics simplicity: hurl everything into a roasting tin, bung into the oven for a few hours and let the magic happen. Of course, to prevent things from drying out or not cooking properly, you need the right set-up. Well, hello, my harissa lamb traybake! The lamb simmers slowly in a rich sauce featuring two of my favourite ingredients – take a bow, ras el hanout and rose harissa – until it's so tender you can pull it apart with a fork. Serve with bulgur or couscous and something crunchy on the side for a truly divine dinner.

SERVES 4

1
Preheat the oven to 200°C/180°C fan/gas 6. Chuck the lamb into a mixing bowl and add the ras el hanout and a good pinch of salt and pepper. Mix well so the meat gets completely coated.

2
Put the onions into a 24x32cm roasting tin and top with the lamb and chickpeas.

3
Whisk together the passata, rose harissa, garlic powder, smoked paprika, a pinch of salt and pepper and 300ml of water. Pour over the lamb and stir together. The meat should be covered by the sauce.

4
Scrunch up some baking paper and wet it under the cold tap. Spread this over the lamb and tuck in the sides. Cover the whole tray with foil and bake for 2 hours. Give everything a good mix. Make sure all the meat is covered in sauce and then cover again with the baking paper and foil. Return to the oven for 1 to 1½ hours or until the meat pulls apart with a fork. Check the seasoning, adding salt to taste, scatter over the coriander leaves and serve immediately.

PREP:
10 minutes

COOK:
3 hours 30 minutes

SMOKY 'NDUJA BOSTON BEANS

- 2 x 400g tins of borlotti beans, drained and rinsed
- 1 stick of celery, finely chopped
- 1 onion, peeled and finely chopped
- ½ a carrot, peeled and finely chopped – or coarsely grated if you can't be bothered
- 6 cloves of garlic, peeled and finely chopped
- 500g tomato passata
- 450ml hot vegetable or chicken stock – from 1 stock cube
- 30g 'nduja paste
- 2 tsp balsamic vinegar
- a bunch of fresh basil
- 80ml olive oil
- salt and pepper

I'm about to share something with the group that's sure to be divisive, but at my age (don't ask!), I'm totally fine owning it: I absolutely loathe baked beans. Always have, always will – they give me the ultimate ick. That said, I can't help but feel a twinge of envy for those nostalgic beans-on-toast moments everyone raves about. So I've created my own version: a smoky, spicy medley made with 'nduja – a fiery Italian pork paste (do check the heat of yours) – tomatoes and a splash of balsamic vinegar. The result? A gloriously hot mess that's smoky, spicy and just a little more elevated than its cousins in the blue tins.

SERVES 4

1
Preheat the oven to 200ºC/180ºC fan/gas 6. Chuck the beans, celery, onion, carrot, garlic, passata, stock, 'nduja, balsamic and plenty of salt and pepper into a 24x32cm roasting tin and stir together.

2
Nestle the basil into the beans and pour over the oil. Scrunch up some baking paper and spread it over the beans, making sure it sits touching them to lock in the moisture. Cover the whole tray with foil and bake for 1 hour 40 minutes to 2 hours in the oven or until the beans are rich and thick.

3
Fish out the basil – it will have done its job so you can now hurl it in the bin. Check the beans for seasoning, adding salt and pepper to taste, and serve. I like to have these glorious baked beans on slices of buttery toast with loads of Parmesan grated over the top.

PREP:
15 minutes

COOK:
2 hours

KOREAN-STYLE BEEF SHORT RIBS

Short ribs are one of the most delicious cuts of meat to use when you have plenty of time to cook them low and slow in the oven. Their chunky, almost rugged appearance might seem daunting at first, but they're surprisingly simple to prepare. Sear them fiercely to achieve a gorgeous golden crust – this caramelization adds so much flavour to the finished dish. Once browned, braise them in a roasting tin with some big flavours like gochujang, soy sauce, rice wine and garlic. The meat becomes so tender that it falls off the bone at the touch of a fork. I like to pile the meat on to a platter, cover it in sauce and rain down loads of vibrant, crunchy toppings. It's a real showstopper.

SERVES 4

2 tbsp groundnut or neutral oil
2kg beef short ribs
4 tbsp rice wine
1 tbsp white wine vinegar
2 tbsp dark soy sauce
2 tsp light soy sauce
3 tbsp gochujang paste – I use a mild one made by Sun Hee
2 tbsp tomato puree
800ml hot chicken stock – from 1 stock cube
1 onion, peeled and roughly sliced
10 cloves of garlic, peeled
a 4–5cm piece of fresh ginger, peeled and sliced
2 tsp caster sugar
2 spring onions, finely sliced
1 red chilli, finely sliced
10g roasted peanuts, roughly chopped
a small handful of roughly torn coriander leaves
salt

1
Preheat the oven to 180°C/160°C fan/gas 4. Heat the oil in a non-stick frying pan over a high heat. Pat the short ribs dry and season them with a little salt – go easy here as you will be adding soy later – then brown them in two batches for 8 to 10 minutes, turning every 2 to 3 minutes until golden. Remove from the pan and put into a 24x32cm roasting tin, fat side up.

2
Meanwhile, whisk the rice wine, vinegar, dark and light soy, gochujang and tomato puree together with the chicken stock.

3
Pop the onion, garlic cloves and ginger into the tin with the short ribs and pour over the stock. The ribs should be about 90% submerged. Scrunch up some baking paper and spread it over the short ribs, making sure it sits touching them to lock in the moisture. Cover the whole tray with foil and roast in the oven for 4 to 4½ hours or until the meat is falling off the bone.

4
Remove the short ribs from the roasting tin, put them into a shallow dish and set to one side. Tip all that amazing sauce from the roasting tin into a saucepan. Add the caster sugar and bring to the boil over a medium heat. Reduce the heat a little and let it bubble away for 15 to 20 minutes until reduced by half. Use a metal spoon to skim off all the fat – there will be a lot.

5
Meanwhile, pull the beef off the bones and remove all the fat. Transfer the meat to a serving dish and keep warm. To serve, drizzle the reduced sauce over the top and scatter over the spring onions, chilli, peanuts and coriander.

PREP: 20 minutes
COOK: 5 hours

Slow Recipes

SLOW-COOKED PULLED PORK TACOS

1kg peeled pineapple

6 cloves of garlic, peeled

2 tbsp chipotle chilli paste – I use Gran Luchito

1 tbsp tomato puree

2 tsp dried oregano

2 tsp ground cumin

2 tsp ground coriander

1.2 kg trimmed pork shoulder, cut into 7.5cm pieces

1 onion, peeled and cut into quarters

3 jalapeño chillies

1 red onion, peeled and finely sliced

juice of 4 limes, plus wedges to serve

2 large handfuls of finely chopped coriander, plus extra to serve

tacos – I use the small corn ones, about 3–4 per person

salt

PREP:
25 minutes

MARINATE:
1 hour

COOK:
3 hours 30 minutes

This fabulous feast is inspired by a classic Mexican dish called *tacos el pastor*: tacos filled with shredded pork that has been marinated in pineapple and dried chillies. The authentic chillies to use are ancho and guajillo, but they are not always easy to find so I use chipotle chilli paste instead. The pork is slow cooked in the marinade until you can pull it apart with two forks.

SERVES 4–6

1
Cut 500g of the pineapple flesh into little chunks and chuck them into a food processor with the garlic cloves, chipotle chilli paste, tomato puree, oregano, cumin, coriander and a pinch of salt. Blitz into a sauce and pour over the pork pieces. Leave to marinate for 1 hour or overnight in the fridge.

2
Preheat the oven to 180°C/160°C fan/gas 4. Put the pork and all the marinade into a 24x32cm roasting tin and mix well. Top with the onion quarters, chillies and the remaining pineapple cut into wedges (take out the tough core). Pour in 100ml of water. The meat should be completely covered. Scrunch up some baking paper and wet it under the cold tap. Spread this over the meat and tuck in the sides. Cover with foil and put into the oven and cook for 3 to 3½ hours or until the meat pulls apart easily with a fork.

3
Meanwhile, mix the red onion slices with the juice of 2 of the limes and a big pinch of salt. Leave to pickle for 20 to 30 minutes, stirring occasionally.

4
Remove the pineapple wedges, onion quarters and chillies from the roasting tin. Shred the meat straight into the sauce, removing any pieces of fat. Add the juice of 1 of the limes and season to taste with salt. Cover and set to one side to keep warm.

5
Finely chop 100g of the pineapple, the onion and 2 or 3 of the chillies, depending on their heat. You can remove the seeds if you like. Chuck the lot into a bowl with the fresh coriander, the juice of the last lime and a pinch of salt and mix well.

6
Serve the pork, pineapple salsa and pickled onions at the table with extra coriander, lime wedges and tacos. I like to load up each taco with plenty of pork, salsa, onions, a squeeze of lime and some ripped coriander.

MOROCCAN LAMB
WITH COUSCOUS

3 preserved lemons
8 cloves of garlic, peeled
juice of 1½ lemons
1 tbsp ras el hanout
2 tbsp olive oil, plus extra for drizzling
1.8kg bone-in lamb shoulder, at room temperature
4 onions, peeled and sliced into rings
350ml white wine
400g giant (pearl) couscous
900ml hot chicken stock – from 1 cube
a handful of finely chopped mint leaves
a handful of finely chopped parsley leaves
300g Greek yoghurt (I use 10% fat)
salt and pepper

PREP:
20 minutes

COOK:
3 hours 55 minutes

Feeding a crowd has never been easier with this spectacular dish. The lamb shoulder is cooked low and slow with fragrant ras el hanout and aromatic preserved lemons until it becomes melt-in-your-mouth tender. As the lamb rests, the fragrant roasting juices are used to flavour the couscous. To serve, pile on a generous handful of fresh herbs and have a dollop of creamy yoghurt on the side.

SERVES 6

1
Preheat the oven to 180ºC/160ºC fan/gas 4. Deseed the preserved lemons and chuck them into a mini chopper. Add the garlic cloves, the juice of 1 lemon, ras el hanout, olive oil and a good pinch of salt and pepper. Blitz until fine, then rub it all over the lamb so it's completely coated.

2
Put the onions into the base of a 30x40cm roasting tin and pop the lamb on top. Pour in the wine and add 300ml of water. Scrunch up some baking paper and wet it under the cold tap. Spread this over the lamb and tuck in the sides. Cover the whole tray with foil and roast for 3 to 3½ hours or until the lamb pulls apart with a fork.

3
Remove the lamb and onions from the roasting dish and set to one side, covered with foil.

4
Remove any burnt bits from the roasting tray and then tip in the couscous. Add the stock and stir together. Put into the oven and cook for 20 to 25 minutes or until the couscous has absorbed all the stock.

5
Just before the couscous is ready, shred the lamb, removing all the fat and bones. Put the meat on to a serving dish, add the onions and a pinch of salt and mix together.

6
Add the remaining lemon juice, most of the mint and parsley and a good drizzle of olive oil to the couscous. Mix well and check the seasoning, adding salt and pepper to taste. Transfer to a serving dish and scatter over the remaining herbs. Serve immediately with the juicy lamb and onions and plenty of yoghurt.

VENISON CHILLI CON CARNE

800g minced venison
1 onion, peeled and finely chopped
1 red pepper, finely chopped
3 cloves of garlic, peeled and finely chopped
2 x 400g tins of chopped tomatoes
1 x 400g tin of kidney beans, drained and rinsed
2 tbsp tomato puree
1 tbsp chipotle chilli paste – I use Gran Luchito
2 tsp dried oregano
1 tsp ground cumin
½ tsp ground cinnamon
60g of 70% dark chocolate, finely chopped
1 tbsp balsamic vinegar
700ml hot beef stock – from 1 stock cube
juice of ½ a lime
300ml soured cream
a handful of roughly chopped coriander
1 red chilli, finely chopped
salt and pepper

Venison's rich, gamy flavour is perfect for this Tex-Mex-style chilli traybake, inspired by classic chilli con carne recipes. The venison is cooked slowly, taking on a spicy kick from the smoky chipotle chilli paste and a velvety richness from a few squares of bitter dark chocolate. As with any slow-cooked meat dish, let it rest for a good 10 minutes so the flavours can really develop before you tuck in.

SERVES 6

1
Preheat the oven to 180°C/160°C fan/gas 4. Pop the venison, onion, pepper, garlic, tomatoes, kidney beans, tomato puree, chipotle chilli paste, oregano, cumin, cinnamon, chocolate, balsamic vinegar, stock and plenty of salt and pepper into a 24x32cm roasting tin. Using a fork, mix everything together. Scrunch up some baking paper and spread it over the venison. Cover the whole tray with foil and roast in the oven for 2½ to 3 hours. Check the chilli after 2½ hours. It should be nice and thick but not dry. If it needs a little more reducing, return to the oven, all covered up, and cook for another 30 minutes, then check again.

2
Once the chilli is perfect, remove from the oven and leave to rest for 10 minutes. This allows all the flavours to really develop. Add the lime juice and mix well. Check the seasoning, adding salt and pepper to taste.

3
Serve the chilli with a dollop of soured cream on the top and garnished with the coriander and red chilli. I like this with long-grain rice and some flatbreads on the side.

PREP:
10 minutes

COOK:
3 hours

CROATIAN-STYLE BEEF PAŠTICADA

One of the many perks of having a Croatian partner is indulging in home-cooked feasts whenever we visit his parents' home in Split. At the top of the must-eat list is always *pašticada*, a hearty stew made with a joint of beef cooked in loads of wine. Traditionally, the slices of beef are served with a thick, velvety gravy and buttery gnocchi. For my version, I use beef shin, which becomes melt-in-your-mouth tender after a long, slow cook. While the classic recipe calls for dried prunes to add sweetness, I never have them at home so I use a splash of balsamic vinegar. The result is a beautifully rich, slightly sweet, tangy, herby and boozy stew that's utterly irresistible. Gnocchi are perfect for soaking up every last bit, but buttery mash or creamy polenta are just as indulgent options.

SERVES 4

800g beef shin, trimmed and cut into 3–5cm pieces

2 tbsp plain flour

1 tbsp Dijon mustard

130g diced pancetta or lardons

1 onion, peeled and finely chopped

1 carrot, peeled and finely chopped

4 cloves of garlic, peeled and finely chopped

2 sprigs of rosemary

2 tbsp tomato puree

500ml hot beef stock – from 1 stock cube

350ml red wine

2 tbsp balsamic vinegar

salt and pepper

1
Preheat the oven to 180°C/160°C fan/gas 4. Chuck the beef into a 24x32cm roasting tin. Add the flour, mustard and a really good pinch of salt and pepper and mix well to coat the meat. Add the pancetta, onion, carrot, garlic, rosemary, tomato puree, beef stock, red wine and balsamic vinegar. Stir together. Scrunch up some baking paper and spread it over the beef, making sure it sits touching the sauce to lock in the moisture. Cover the whole tray with foil and put into the oven and cook for 3 to 3½ hours or until the meat is lovely and tender.

2
Remove the foil from the roasting tin. Poke a few holes into the baking paper, making sure it's still snug over the meat. This will stop it from drying out and let the sauce reduce at the same time. Return to the oven for 30 to 40 minutes or until the sauce is lovely and thick. Check the seasoning, adding salt and pepper to taste, and serve immediately.

PREP:
15 minutes

COOK:
4 hours 10 minutes

LEBANESE-LANCASHIRE HOT POT

1kg boneless lamb neck fillets, cut into 2–3cm pieces
2 tbsp plain flour
2 tsp baharat
1 tsp ground cinnamon
2 onions, peeled and finely chopped
4 cloves of garlic, peeled and finely chopped
1 large aubergine, cut into 2cm pieces
1 x 400g tin of chopped tomatoes
2 tsp dried thyme
800ml hot lamb stock – from 1 stock cube
2 tbsp tomato puree
1 tbsp Worcester sauce
1kg potatoes, peeled and sliced into ¼cm rounds
1 tbsp olive oil
salt and pepper

This dish is a delightful mash-up, a British classic fused with a dusting of Lebanese magic. While I adore a traditional Lancashire lamb hotpot, to my palate it's often a little bland. So I've had a tinker and added in some aubergine and a medley of spices – it's loosely based on the stews I had when I was travelling around Lebanon. The oven does all the hard work, slow cooking the lamb until it's meltingly tender. The end result is a rich and deeply savoury stew with the most irresistibly soft and slightly charred potato topping.

SERVES 6

1
Preheat the oven to 180ºC/160ºC fan/gas 4. Pop the lamb into a mixing bowl and add the flour, baharat, cinnamon and plenty of salt and pepper. Toss together and chuck into a 30x40cm roasting tin. Add the onions, garlic, aubergine, tinned tomatoes and thyme.

2
Whisk together the stock, tomato puree, Worcester sauce and plenty of salt and pepper. Pour into the roasting tin and stir together. The lamb should be nearly covered. Scrunch up some baking paper and spread it over the lamb. Cover the whole tray with foil and roast for 3 hours until the lamb is tender.

3
Meanwhile, put the potato slices into a bowl of cold water and let them sit for 10 minutes to get some of the starch out. Drain well and pat dry.

4
Give the lamb a good mix and check the seasoning, adding salt to taste. Pour in 200ml of water – don't worry about stirring it – and then layer the potatoes over the top. Drizzle over the olive oil and season with loads of salt. Cover with just foil and roast for 30 minutes, then remove the foil and cook for another 40 to 50 minutes or until the top is golden and bubbling around the edges. Leave it to rest for 5 to 10 minutes, so the flavours can develop, before serving.

PREP:
25 minutes

COOK:
4 hours 20 minutes

SLOW-COOKED COCONUT BEEF CURRY

for the curry paste:

3 stalks of lemongrass

4 mild long red chillies, deseeded as you like and roughly chopped

4 shallots, halved

a 4–5cm piece of fresh ginger, peeled and roughly chopped

4 cloves of garlic, peeled

2 tsp ground coriander

1 tsp ground cumin

salt

for the curry:

1kg beef shin, cut into 2–3cm pieces

800ml coconut milk

juice of 1½ limes, plus wedges to serve

1 tbsp fish sauce

1 tsp dark soy

6–8 fresh lime leaves

4 cardamom pods

1 star anise

a few coriander leaves

20g roasted peanuts, crushed

2 red chillies, finely sliced

This meltingly soft, fragrant and tangy beef curry takes inspiration from the legendary Indonesian beef rendang, often hailed as one of the world's greatest curries. I have borrowed a few elements to make this indulgent traybake that cooks low and slow in a vibrant curry paste, with some added aromatics and coconut milk. To strike the perfect mellow hum, I use four mild chillies, deseeding two to keep some heat, which I top up with freshly chopped red chillies when I serve.

SERVES 6

1

Preheat the oven to 180°C/160°C fan/gas 4. To make the spice paste, cut the woody stalks off the lemongrass and throw them into a 24x32cm roasting tin for later. Remove the tough outer layer and discard that. Roughly chop the rest and put the pieces into a mini chopper with the chillies, shallots, ginger, garlic cloves, ground coriander, cumin, a pinch of salt and 4 tablespoons of water. Blitz into a fine paste.

2

Pop the beef into the roasting tin with the lemongrass stalks, season with salt and mix well. Add the curry paste and mix so that all the meat is coated, then add the coconut milk, lime juice, fish sauce, soy, lime leaves, cardamom pods and star anise. Stir together. Scrunch up some baking paper and spread it over the beef, making sure it sits touching the sauce to lock in the moisture. Cover the whole tray with foil and put into the oven and cook for 2 hours.

3

Remove the roasting tin from the oven and take off the foil. Poke a few holes into the middle of the baking paper to let the steam out and allow the sauce to reduce, but make sure it's very snug over the meat to stop it from drying out. Return to the oven for 1½ to 2 hours or until the sauce is rich and thick and the beef meltingly tender.

4

Let the beef rest for 5 minutes and then spoon off the excess fat. Give the sauce a good mix. You can remove the aromatics at this point. Serve immediately with the coriander, peanuts, chillies and lime wedges at the table. I like to pair this with loads of fluffy rice.

PREP:
15 minutes

COOK:
4 hours

GREEK-ISH LAMB STIFADO

1 tbsp groundnut or neutral oil

1kg lamb shoulder, cut into 5cm pieces

700ml hot lamb stock – from 1 stock cube

2 tbsp tomato puree

1 tsp sugar

1½ tsp ground cinnamon

¾ tsp allspice

150g shallots, peeled and larger ones halved

8 cloves of garlic, peeled

2 sprigs of rosemary

1 x 400g tin of chopped tomatoes

salt and pepper

Meltingly tender lamb in a simple but flavourful sauce of tomatoes, garlic, cinnamon and allspice, this is my take on the quintessentially Greek recipe lamb *stifado*. I adore this kind of lazy cooking where the oven does all the heavy lifting. Now, here's a little secret. The traditional recipes use small shallots but I find peeling them uber fiddly, so if I'm in a rush I grab peeled frozen baby onions from the supermarket and throw them straight into the roasting tin instead. If you can make life easier for yourself, why would you not?

SERVES 4

1
Preheat the oven to 180ºC/160ºC fan/gas 4. Heat the oil in a non-stick frying pan and season the lamb all over with loads of salt and pepper. Brown the meat for 2 to 3 minutes each side until really golden all over. You'll need to do this in three batches so that the pan is never overcrowded. Transfer the cooked lamb to a 24x32cm roasting tin.

2
Whisk together the stock, tomato puree, sugar, cinnamon and allspice and pour over the lamb. Add the shallots, garlic cloves, rosemary, tinned tomatoes and pinch of salt and pepper and stir together. Scrunch up some baking paper and spread it over the lamb. Cover the whole tray with foil and pop into the oven for 2 to 2½ hours until the meat is soft and tender.

3
Remove the foil and poke a few holes into the middle of the baking paper to let the steam out and help reduce the sauce. Make sure it's very snug over the meat to stop it from drying out. Return to the oven for 30 to 40 minutes or until the sauce has reduced and is lovely and thick. Check the seasoning, adding salt and pepper to taste. Skim off any excess fat and once you're happy serve immediately. I like this with bulgur wheat or buttery orzo.

PREP:
12 minutes

COOK:
3 hours 30 minutes

STICKY SOY AND GINGER PORK BELLY

1 tbsp groundnut or neutral oil

1kg pork belly slices

800ml hot chicken stock – from 1 stock cube

4 tbsp rice wine

2 tbsp dark soy sauce

2 tbsp oyster sauce

2 tbsp light brown sugar

4 spring onions, roughly chopped, plus 2 more, finely sliced, to garnish

4 cloves of garlic, peeled

a 4–5cm piece of fresh ginger, peeled and cut into strips

1 tbsp sesame seeds

1 tsp Szechuan peppercorns

1 tsp chilli flakes

salt

This heavenly, slow-cooked sticky soy and ginger pork belly traybake is really something special. The pork braises low and slow in a wonderfully aromatic sauce. You literally don't have to do anything more than leave it alone. Over time, the meat becomes meltingly tender, while the sauce thickens into a rich, sweet and salty glaze that's intense in all the right ways. To cut through the richness of the unctuous pork, I love sprinkling a tongue-tingling mix of ground Szechuan peppercorns and spicy chilli flakes over the top when serving.

SERVES 4

1
Preheat the oven to 180°C/160°C fan/gas 4 and heat the oil in a large non-stick frying pan over a high heat. Add the pork slices to the frying pan and brown for 3 to 4 minutes each side. (You may have to do this in batches.) Remove from the pan and put into a 24x32cm roasting tin and shake together.

2
Whisk together the stock, rice wine, soy sauce, oyster sauce and sugar and pour over the pork. Add the chopped spring onions, garlic cloves and ginger to the tin.

3
Scrunch up some baking paper and spread it over the pork, making sure it sits tightly over the top to keep the pork submerged in the stock. Cover the whole tray with foil and put into the oven for 2 hours. Remove the foil, leaving the baking paper in place, and return the tin to the oven for 1 hour. The meat will be very tender by this stage.

4
Turn the pork over in the sauce and baste it well. Cover again with the baking paper and return to the oven for 30 to 40 minutes or until the sauce is lovely and thick. Baste the pork well and scatter over the sesame seeds and sliced spring onions.

5
Meanwhile, grind the Szechuan peppercorns together with the chilli flakes and serve immediately in a little bowl alongside the pork. I recommend having this with piles of rice to soak up the lovely juices.

PREP:
8 minutes

COOK:
4 hours

IRAQI-STYLE STUFFED ONIONS

4 onions
4 cloves of garlic, peeled
a handful of finely chopped coriander leaves, plus a few extra leaves, to garnish
600g minced beef – I use 20% fat
3 tsp baharat
½ tsp ground cinnamon
1l hot beef stock – from 1 stock cube
1 x 400g tin of chopped tomatoes
2 tbsp tomato puree
1 tbsp pomegranate molasses
salt and pepper

PREP:
20 minutes

COOK:
2 hours 25 minutes

Dolma is a classic Middle Eastern dish of vegetables stuffed with spiced rice and sometimes ground meat. This particular version is called *dolma mahshi* or onion dolma. There's no rice required. Instead, layers are peeled off the onions and stuffed with an intensely spiced beef mince, then slow cooked until super soft in a tangy sweet tomato and pomegranate sauce.

SERVES 4

1
Preheat the oven to 200ºC/180ºC fan/gas 6. Top and tail the onions and peel them. Make a cut right into the centre so you can separate the layers of the onion. I find that pushing out some of the little bits around the core loosens it all up and then you can wiggle the outer layers off. You want 4 layers from each onion. Don't worry if they rip a little.

2
Put the inner bits of the onions into a food processor. Add the garlic and coriander and give everything a good blitz until fine. Add the beef, 2 teaspoons of the baharat, a quarter-teaspoon of the ground cinnamon and a big pinch of salt and pepper. Pulse together.

3
Stuff the 16 onion layers with the meat filling, squeezing them tight to close them up. Arrange them on their sides in a 24x32cm roasting tin.

4
Whisk together the stock, chopped tomatoes, tomato puree, pomegranate molasses, the remaining teaspoon of baharat and quarter-teaspoon of cinnamon and plenty of salt and pepper. Pour over the onions. Scrunch up some baking paper and spread it over the onions, making sure it sits touching them to keep them submerged. Cover the whole tray with foil and roast in the oven for 1 hour 45 minutes to 2 hours until the onions are super tender.

5
Remove the onions from the sauce and transfer to a serving dish, cover and set to one side. Pour the sauce into a saucepan and bring to the boil over a high heat. Cook, stirring occasionally, for 20 to 25 minutes until the sauce has reduced by well over half.

6
Drain any liquid from the resting onions, then pour the thickened sauce over them. Scatter over a few ripped coriander leaves and serve immediately. This is great with rice and salads.

CRISPY GNOCCHI WITH BURRATA AND GREEN PESTO	166
ROASTED MUSHROOM RISOTTO	168
QUICK-COOK LAMB RAGU	170
LAMB BIRYANI-ISH WITH MINTY YOGHURT DRIZZLE	172
SPEEDY CHEESY RAVIOLI BAKE	174
PRAWN AND ORZO FIDEUÀ	176
SPICY 'NDUJA CANNELLONI	178
COCONUT CHILLI BEEF RICE	180
COSY GNOCCHI AND BACON GRATIN	182
SUMMERY ORZO WITH CREAMY BURRATA	184
BAKED ITALIAN RISOTTO	186
CREAMY GORGONZOLA AND BUTTERNUT SQUASH STUFFED PASTA SHELLS	188
THE GREATEST CHORIZO BAKED RICE	190
PRAWN AND FETA ORZO	192
CARAMELIZED ONION PASTA BAKE	194
GOOEY GOCHUJANG MAC CHEESE	196

RICE AND PASTA RECIPES

Welcome to carb heaven. A safe place, packed with mouth-watering meals for those times when you need something comforting to eat. The ooze factor here is off the charts. There is never any judgement, just pure enjoyment. No matter what you fancy or how much time you have to linger in the kitchen, you'll find the perfect dish to satisfy your cravings. So sit back and get ready for a feast.

CRISPY GNOCCHI
WITH BURRATA AND GREEN PESTO

3 tbsp olive oil, plus extra for greasing

1 x 500g pack gnocchi

400g cherry tomatoes, most halved

½ a red onion, peeled and roughly chopped

100g chorizo, finely chopped

a 30g bunch of fresh basil

½ a clove of garlic, peeled

juice of ¼ of a lemon

20g Parmesan cheese, roughly chopped

15g pine nuts

150g burrata, at room temperature

salt and pepper

I am fully obsessed with gnocchi traybakes, and if you haven't tried one yet, this is your sign to dive in. It couldn't be easier: start with shop-bought gnocchi and toss them straight into a roasting tin – no need to pre-boil! – with tomatoes, onion and chorizo. As it bakes, the onion and tomatoes create a rich sauce that makes the gnocchi soft and tender on the bottom, while the top turns golden and crispy, with the chorizo melting though everything. Finish off with creamy burrata and green pesto to turn it into such a special meal.

SERVES 2

1
Preheat the oven to 200ºC/180ºC fan/gas 6. Rub a little oil all over the base of a 24x32cm roasting tin. Chuck in the gnocchi, cherry tomatoes and red onion. Add 1 tablespoon of the oil and plenty of salt and pepper. Toss together. Scatter the chorizo over the top and pour over 80ml of water. Pop into the oven for 30 to 35 minutes or until the top is crispy and the bottom soft.

2
Meanwhile, make the pesto by blitzing the basil, garlic, lemon juice, Parmesan, pine nuts, the remaining 2 tablespoons of oil, 1 tablespoon of water and plenty of salt and pepper in a food processor. Blast it, scraping down the sides occasionally, for a few minutes until really creamy.

3
Rip the burrata over the gnocchi and spoon over the pesto. Grab a fork and tuck in.

PREP:
15 minutes

COOK:
35 minutes

ROASTED MUSHROOM RISOTTO

600g fresh mushrooms, finely sliced – I use a mix of chestnut, portobello and shitake

3 tbsp olive oil, plus extra for drizzling

1 tsp dried thyme

10g dried porcini mushrooms

400ml just-boiled water

300g Arborio rice

2 cloves of garlic, peeled and crushed

700ml hot chicken or vegetable stock – from 1 stock cube

100ml white wine

30g butter, cubed

30g grated Parmesan cheese (or vegetarian alternative), plus extra for serving

juice of ¼ of a lemon

a small handful of finely chopped chives

salt and pepper

PREP:
15 minutes

COOK:
1 hour 10 minutes

Hands up if you love a gorgeously creamy risotto. Now, keep that hand up if you're not a fan of the constant stirring that comes with making it. Thought so. Let's face it, it's not difficult, just a bit dull. Well, my traybake makes creating an impressive risotto a doddle. You roast off the mushrooms in the oven until they're charred and intense and use that as the base to flavour the rice. Once cooked, finish it off by stirring in heaps of butter and cheese for that ultimate ooze factor.

SERVES 4

1
Preheat the oven to 220ºC/200ºC fan/gas 7. Chuck all the fresh mushrooms into a 30x40cm roasting tin. Add the oil, thyme and plenty of salt and pepper. Toss together and roast for 25 to 30 minutes or until the mushrooms are charred and tender. Remove from the roasting tin and set to one side.

2
Meanwhile, soak the dried porcini in 200ml of just-boiled water and leave to infuse for 15 minutes. Remove the porcini with a spoon, reserving the liquid, and finely chop them.

3
Reduce the oven to 200ºC/180ºC fan/gas 6. Tip the rice into the roasting tin and add the finely chopped porcini and the soaking water, garlic, chicken stock and wine. Stir together and cover with foil. Put into the oven for 35 to 40 minutes or until the rice has absorbed all the liquid and is al dente.

4
Remove the foil and add the butter, Parmesan, lemon juice, most of the chives and plenty of salt and pepper. Mix well. Add in 150–200ml of just-boiled water and stir together for 1 to 2 minutes or until the rice starts to go creamy. Check the seasoning, adding salt and pepper to taste. Add half the mushrooms and stir together. If the rice needs it, you can cover the tin and return it to the oven for a few minutes to warm through, then stir through a splash of just-boiled water to make it go creamy before serving.

5
To serve, divide the rice between four plates. Top with the remaining mushrooms, the remaining chives and plenty of grated Parm. Drizzle over a little oil and dive in.

Rice and Pasta Recipes

QUICK-COOK LAMB RAGU

6 tomatoes (about 400g)
2 tbsp tomato puree
3 cloves of garlic, peeled and crushed
2 tsp dried oregano
2 tsp Turkish pepper flakes
500g minced lamb – I use 20% fat
1 tbsp groundnut or neutral oil
500g fresh lasagna sheets
200ml double cream
Parmesan cheese, grated, to serve
salt and pepper

There is nothing more comforting than a creamy pasta ragu, and this wickedly indulgent quick-cook version makes a divine midweek meal. The lamb is roasted in the oven with loads of garlic and tomatoes until golden and crispy, then you stir in plenty of cream and cheese to lux it up. Instead of regular pasta, I use fresh lasagna sheets, cutting them into big, rustic pieces. They cook in minutes, keeping things speedy, and their silky texture gives this dish a restaurant-quality vibe.

SERVES 4–6

1
Preheat the oven to 240°C/220°C fan/gas 9. Using the coarse side of a cheese grater, grate the tomatoes over a shallow dish. Keep the pulp and discard the skins. Add the tomato puree, garlic, dried oregano, Turkish pepper flakes and a good pinch of salt and pepper. Mix well.

2
Put the lamb into a 30x40cm non-stick or lined roasting tin. Add the oil and a good pinch of salt and mix well. Chuck in the tomato mix and pour in 200ml of water. Mix and spread out evenly. Pop into the oven for 15 minutes. Take it out and give it a good mix, then return to the oven for another 12 to 15 minutes or until the sauce is clinging to the lamb, which is starting to go crispy at the edges.

3
Meanwhile, place the lasagna sheets on a chopping board so they are landscape. Cut vertically into three pieces, so you have wide pieces of pasta. Cook them for 2 to 3 minutes in a large pan of boiling water until al dente. Scoop out and reserve some of the pasta water, then drain.

4
Add the double cream to the lamb and mix well. Add the pasta and 50–100ml of the pasta water – start with 50ml and see how you go. Mix until creamy and check the seasoning, adding salt and pepper to taste. Rain down a load of Parm and serve immediately.

PREP:
15 minutes

COOK:
30 minutes

LAMB BIRYANI-ISH
WITH MINTY YOGHURT DRIZZLE

650g leg of lamb, all fat removed, cut into 2–3cm pieces

500g Greek yoghurt (I use 10% fat)

juice of 1 lemon

2 tsp ground cumin

2 tsp garam masala

½ tsp chilli powder

4 cloves of garlic, peeled and crushed

a 2–3cm piece of fresh ginger, peeled and grated

300g basmati rice

600ml lamb stock, from one stock cube

1 tbsp lime pickle

70g butter

a pinch of saffron

a large handful of finely chopped mint leaves, plus a few extra leaves, to garnish

20g flaked almonds

salt and pepper

PREP:
15 minutes

MARINATE:
1 hour

COOK:
40 minutes

Inspired by the magnificent Indian biryani, this elevated traybake makes an impressive centrepiece for any dinner party. The lamb is tenderized in yoghurt, lemon and warming spices – make sure you remove all the fat from the lamb otherwise it will be chewy – and then cooked with fragrant basmati rice and a cheeky drizzle of saffron butter. No saffron in the cupboard? No worries. Just swap it for 1 teaspoon of paprika instead.

SERVES 4

1
Chuck the lamb into a mixing bowl and add 100g of the yoghurt. Add the lemon juice, cumin, garam masala, chilli powder, garlic, ginger and a good pinch of salt and pepper. Mix well, then cover and refrigerate for an hour or overnight.

2
Preheat the oven to 220°C/200°C fan/gas 7 and get the lamb to room temperature. Transfer the lamb and all the marinade to a 24x32cm roasting tin and tip over the rice.

3
Whisk together the lamb stock, lime pickle and a pinch of salt. Pour over the rice. Shake the tray so the meat and rice are covered by the stock. Cover with foil and roast for 25 to 30 minutes until all the liquid has been absorbed by the rice.

4
Meanwhile, melt the butter in a little saucepan over a medium heat. Add the saffron and swirl around. Remove from the heat and leave to infuse for a few minutes.

5
Drizzle the saffron butter over the rice. Cover and return to the oven. Now you're going to turn the heat off and leave the roasting tin in there for 10 minutes so the residual heat will finish cooking the rice slowly.

6
While the rice finishes cooking, mix the remaining 400g yoghurt with the mint and a pinch of salt.

7
When you're ready, check the seasoning, adding salt to taste. Scatter over the almonds and tear over some mint leaves. Serve immediately with the yoghurt on the side.

Rice and Pasta Recipes

Let's be honest, this isn't haute cuisine and it's not trying to be. This is pure, unpretentious comfort food: simple, satisfying and ready in minutes. Perfect for those chaotic Monday nights after a long day at work or when you've accidentally had one too many vinos on a Friday night. Enter my speedy, cheesy ravioli bake. Layers of shop-bought pasta, rich tomato sauce and plenty of gooey, melted cheese. It's exactly what I want when I am cooking at home in the week. Nothing fancy or fiddly. Feel free to use any fresh ravioli you like. I love a spinach and ricotta, and the cheese and ham ones are a massive guilty pleasure for me. You do you and use whatever you love.

SPEEDY CHEESY RAVIOLI BAKE

1 tbsp olive oil
700g tomato passata
2 tbsp tomato puree
2 tsp garlic powder
2 tsp dried oregano
500g fresh ravioli
160g grated mozzarella (from a bag or the firm stuff)
200ml just-boiled water
salt and pepper

SERVES 4

1
Preheat the oven to 220°C/200°C fan/gas 7. Rub the olive oil all over a 24x32cm roasting tin.

2
Whisk together the tomato passata, tomato puree, garlic powder, dried oregano and a large pinch of salt and pepper. Spoon a few tablespoons into the roasting tin and spread out all over the bottom to stop the pasta sticking.

3
Layer up half the ravioli in the roasting tin. I'm a real neat freak so I like nice lines but feel free to do it your way. Spoon over half the tomato sauce and sprinkle over half the cheese. Add the remaining ravioli (in fun lines if you like!), then spoon over the remaining sauce.

4
Pour 200ml of just-boiled water into the roasting tin and gently push the ravioli down into the sauce so they're just covered. Sprinkle over the remaining cheese and cover with foil. Put into the oven and cook for 10 minutes to soften the ravioli.

5
Remove the foil and return the ravioli to the oven to roast for 10 to 12 minutes so the cheese can melt and go all oozy. Serve immediately.

PREP:
8 minutes

COOK:
22 minutes

PRAWN AND ORZO FIDEUÀ

350g orzo

4 cloves of garlic, peeled and finely chopped

580ml hot chicken stock – from 1 stock cube

juice of 1 lemon, plus wedges to serve

4 tbsp sun-dried tomato paste

3 tsp smoked paprika

½ tsp chilli flakes

30g butter, cubed

300g raw peeled king prawns

1 tbsp olive oil

a handful of roughly chopped parsley leaves

garlic mayonnaise or aioli, to serve

salt and pepper

This dish takes inspiration from Spanish *fideuà*, a paella of sorts made with broken vermicelli pasta, cooked until soft in some parts and crispy in others. Orzo is a simple swap that's easier to find and works just as beautifully. The orzo is simmered in a rich, intensely flavoured stock until tender and golden and crispy at the edges. It's topped off with juicy prawns – you can add squid and mussels if you like – and finished off with a squeeze of lemon to make the whole thing pop and a dollop of garlic mayo (or traditional aioli) over the top.

SERVES 4

1
Preheat the oven to 200°C/180°C fan/gas 6 and chuck the orzo and garlic into a 30x40cm non-stick or lined roasting tin.

2
Whisk the stock together with half the lemon juice, the sun-dried tomato paste, smoked paprika, chilli flakes and plenty of salt and pepper. Pour over the orzo and mix well. Cover the tin with foil and put into the oven for 15 minutes so the orzo can absorb all the liquid. Remove the foil and dot the butter over the top. Return to the oven for 10 to 15 minutes or until the orzo is starting to go crispy at the sides.

3
Meanwhile, put the prawns into a mixing bowl and add the olive oil and a pinch of salt. Scatter the prawns over the top of the orzo and return to the oven for 3 to 5 minutes or until they are just cooked through. Add the remaining lemon juice and scatter over the parsley. Serve immediately with a dollop of garlic mayonnaise or aioli and lemon wedges on the side.

PREP:
10 minutes

COOK:
35 minutes

SPICY 'NDUJA CANNELLONI

200g pork sausages, skins removed
60g 'nduja paste
250g mascarpone
300g fresh lasagna sheets, at room temperature (at least 30 minutes out of the fridge)
1 x 400g tin of chopped tomatoes
2 tbsp tomato puree
2 tsp garlic powder
1 tsp dried oregano
150g cheese, grated – I like a mix of Cheddar and mozzarella
salt

This seriously impressive traybake gives off major nonna vibes: stuffed cannelloni that feel homemade, but you'll be using fresh pasta sheets as a shortcut – no judgement here! The filling is a flavourful blend of sausage meat, mascarpone and spicy 'nduja paste, one of my all-time favourite ingredients. 'Nduja is a cured pork spread, made with fiery chillies, that packs a serious punch. Sure, rolling the cannelloni up takes a little time, but pour yourself a glass of vino, crank up the tunes and have fun with it. Besides, those fresh pasta sheets bake in no time, getting crispy on the edges and beautifully gooey in the middle.

SERVES 4

1
Preheat the oven to 200°C/180°C fan/gas 6. Put the sausage meat and 'nduja paste into a mixing bowl and mash together with a fork. Add the mascarpone and a pinch of salt and stir to combine.

2
Cut the lasagna sheets in half widthways so you have two smaller shaped rectangles. Lay one half out like a portrait picture, then place a generous tablespoon of the mixture at the bottom end, spread it out and roll the pasta up tight into a cigar shape. I find a tiny bit of the mixture helps to seal it shut. Repeat with the rest, placing the rolls fold side down into a 24x32cm roasting tin in neat rows.

3
Mix the tinned tomatoes together with the tomato puree, 200ml of water, garlic powder, oregano and a pinch of salt. Pour over the pasta and top with the cheese. Bake for 20 to 25 minutes or until golden and bubbly. Pull it out of the oven and let it rest for 5 to 10 minutes before serving.

PREP:
20 minutes

COOK:
25 minutes

COCONUT CHILLI BEEF RICE

500g minced beef – I use 10–12% fat

1 onion, peeled and finely chopped

2 tbsp groundnut or neutral oil

400ml hot chicken stock – from 1 stock cube

3 cloves of garlic, peeled and crushed

2 tbsp oyster sauce

1 tbsp fish sauce

1 tbsp dark soy sauce

1 tbsp sriracha – or chilli sauce of choice

300g basmati rice

200ml coconut milk

juice of ½ a lime

3 spring onions, finely chopped

a handful of finely chopped coriander leaves

optional: crispy fried onions, to serve

salt

Get ready to have this lip-smackingly good coconut chilli beef rice on your weekly dinner rotation. Crispy beef is cooked with rice in an umami-packed stock and topped with golden, crunchy fried onions. I'm going to fully admit it: I buy crispy fried onions ready to rock in a pot – you get instant flavour and no gross deep frying. There are a lot of salty condiments going on here. If you're using regular soy sauce rather than the less salty dark soy, start with just a teaspoon in the stock. You can always add more at the end.

SERVES 4

1
Preheat the oven to 220ºC/200ºC fan/gas 7. Chuck the beef, onion, oil and a little pinch of salt into a 24x32cm roasting tin. Mix well to break up the beef and then arrange in an even layer. Roast in the oven for 20 to 25 minutes or until the beef is a little crispy.

2
Meanwhile, whisk together the stock, garlic, oyster sauce, fish sauce, soy and sriracha.

3
Break the beef up with a fork. Add the rice and pour over the stock and coconut milk. Stir together and cover with foil. Put into the oven for 20 to 25 minutes or until all the liquid is absorbed, then turn the heat off and leave in the oven for 10 minutes so the residual heat will finish cooking the rice slowly.

4
Add the lime juice, spring onions and coriander and fork them through the rice. Garnish with loads of crispy onions, if using, and serve immediately.

PREP:
12 minutes

COOK:
1 hour

COSY GNOCCHI AND BACON GRATIN

500g gnocchi
60g cubed pancetta or bacon
1 tbsp olive oil
120ml white wine
150ml double cream
1 small clove of garlic, peeled and crushed
1 tsp Dijon mustard
100g Gouda cheese, grated
20g Parmesan cheese, finely grated
salt and pepper

Sometimes life is not all peachy, and when it throws you lemons, particularly if you've had a crap week at work or a rather wild weekend – by mistake of course – pop them into a fruit bowl and save them for next time. Instead, whip up this indulgent gnocchi and bacon gratin. It's a literal food hug in a roasting tin. Golden gnocchi and little crispy bits of pancetta, bubbling away in a creamy, cheesy sauce. For what it's worth, my suggestion would be to grab yourself a big old bowl of this glorious dish, pour a glass of wine and sink into a trashy box set on the sofa. Heaven or what?

SERVES 2

1
Preheat the oven to 200ºC/180ºC fan/gas 6. Chuck the gnocchi and bacon into a 24x32cm roasting tin, add the oil and a pinch of salt and pepper and mix well. Pour in the wine and roast for 18 to 20 minutes until the gnocchi are a little golden.

2
Meanwhile, pour the double cream into a jug and add the garlic, mustard, 50g of the Gouda, all the Parmesan, 100ml of water and a pinch of salt and pepper and whisk it all together.

3
Pour the sauce over the gnocchi. Scatter over the remaining Gouda and return to the oven for 15 to 20 minutes or until golden and bubbly. If you can bear to, I suggest leaving it to cool down for a few minutes before serving, so you don't burn your mouth.

PREP:
5 minutes

COOK:
40 minutes

SUMMERY ORZO
WITH CREAMY BURRATA

1 courgette, cut into 0.5cm cubes
150g asparagus, cut into 1cm pieces
1 tbsp olive oil, plus extra for drizzling
150g frozen peas
120g roasted artichoke hearts in oil, drained
700ml hot vegetable stock – from 1 stock cube
4 tbsp green pesto
400g orzo
juice of ½ a lemon
80ml just-boiled water
150–200g burrata, at room temperature
salt and pepper

I'm very much a pasta-all-year kind of guy. In the summer, I like a lighter dish, but I still crave something creamy and indulgent from time to time and this orzo traybake delivers just that. A healthy dose of heavenly seasonal vegetables – courgette, asparagus, peas and artichokes – finished off with creamy burrata that melts luxuriously over everything. It makes a fabulous dinner for a warm summer evening, best enjoyed with a crisp glass of rosé. Now, if you want that awesome ooze factor from your burrata, be sure to take it out of the fridge a few hours before it's required.

SERVES 4

1
Preheat the oven to 220°C/200°C fan/gas 7. Put the courgette and asparagus into a 24x32cm roasting tin. Add the olive oil and plenty of salt and pepper. Mix well and pop into the oven for 10 minutes to start them cooking. Then add the peas and artichokes, mix well and return to the oven for 5 minutes to get some heat into everything.

2
Meanwhile, whisk the stock together with the pesto.

3
Take the vegetables out of the oven and reduce the heat to 200°C/180°C fan/gas 6. Pour in the stock and add the orzo and stir well. Scrunch up some baking paper and spread it over the orzo and veg, making sure it's touching the stock to lock in the moisture. Cook for 10 to 12 minutes or until the orzo has absorbed all the liquid and is al dente.

4
Stir in the lemon juice and check the seasoning, adding salt and pepper to taste.

5
When you're ready to serve, splash 80ml of just-boiled water into the orzo and mix it well. This will wake it up and turn it really creamy. Transfer to your serving dish and rip over the burrata. It should ooze all over the top. Drizzle over some olive oil, season and serve immediately.

PREP:
12 minutes

COOK:
27 minutes

BAKED ITALIAN RISOTTO

500g minced beef – I use 12–15% fat

1 onion, peeled and finely chopped

4 cloves of garlic, peeled and crushed

2 tsp dried oregano

1 tsp chilli flakes

2 tbsp tomato puree

2 x 400g tins of chopped tomatoes

500ml hot beef stock – from 1 stock cube

200g risotto rice

a large handful of roughly chopped basil leaves

220g scamorza, grated – or use firm mozzarella

50g Parmesan cheese, grated

salt and pepper

Hailing from the sun-soaked Campania region of southern Italy, this wonderful *riso al forno* feels like the love child of a lasagna and a risotto, and I am so here for it. Risotto rice takes the place of pasta, soaking up all the rich flavours of a hearty beef ragu. A healthy amount of cheese is sprinkled over the top of the dish to go gorgeously golden as it bakes. Traditionally the recipe calls for scamorza, a smoky, slightly firmer cousin of mozzarella, which adds a lovely depth. If you can find it, it's a game-changer, but regular mozzarella works beautifully too.

SERVES 6

1
Preheat the oven to 200°C/180°C fan/gas 6. Chuck the beef, onion, garlic, oregano, chilli flakes, tomato puree and a big pinch of salt and pepper into a 24x32cm roasting tin. Grab a fork and break the beef up. Pour in the tinned tomatoes and beef stock and mix well. Cover the tin with foil and pop into the oven for 1 hour. This will get all the flavours of the ragu going and really soften the onion. Remove the foil and return to the oven for 30 minutes to let the sauce thicken a little.

2
When the meat is nearly ready, boil the rice for 8 minutes in a large pan of salted boiling water. Drain well.

3
Add the rice, the basil and two-thirds of both the scamorza and Parmesan to the roasting tin. Mix well and have a little taste to check the seasoning, adding salt and pepper to taste. Top with the remaining cheese and return to the oven for 25 to 30 minutes until the top is golden and the rice cooked through. Cover the dish and let it rest for 10 minutes to firm up before serving.

PREP:
12 minutes

COOK:
2 hours

CREAMY GORGONZOLA
AND BUTTERNUT SQUASH STUFFED PASTA SHELLS

600g peeled butternut squash, cut into 1cm cubes
2 tbsp olive oil
16 giant pasta shells (conchiglioni)
110g gorgonzola (or dolcelatte as a vegetarian alternative)
30g Parmesan cheese (or vegetarian alternative), grated, plus extra for the topping
1 medium free-range egg
650g tomato passata
2 tsp dried oregano
1 tsp garlic powder
120g mozzarella
salt and pepper

PREP:
25 minutes

COOK:
1 hour 30 minutes

This dreamy traybake is the perfect combination of comfort and sophistication: giant pasta shells brimming with an indulgent filling of butternut squash, creamy gorgonzola and Parmesan. If you want to make it fully vegetarian, switch these out for dolcelatte and a vegetarian Italian hard cheese. The pasta is nestled into a rich tomato sauce and baked with more cheese on top. While it does take some time to throw together, you can get ahead by prepping everything up to the point of adding the sauce well ahead of time.

SERVES 4

1
Preheat the oven to 200°C/180°C fan/gas 6. Pop the squash into a 24x32cm roasting tin and add the olive oil and a pinch of salt and pepper. Mix well and roast for 30 to 35 minutes or until just tender. Turn the oven off, take out the squash and transfer to a plate. Put this into the fridge for 10 to 15 minutes so the squash can cool.

2
Meanwhile, boil the pasta for 10 minutes or 3 minutes less than directed on the back of the packet. Drain well and give a quick rinse with cold water to make them easier to hold.

3
Once the squash is cool, mash until smooth and then add the gorgonzola, Parmesan, egg and plenty of salt and pepper. Stir together until combined.

4
Preheat the oven to 200°C/180°C fan/gas 6 again. Pour the tomato passata into the roasting tin and add the oregano, garlic powder and a good pinch of salt and pepper. Mix well.

5
Fill each pasta shell with the squash mixture, then nestle them into the sauce leaving a little room around each one as they will expand in the oven. Rip the mozzarella over the top and cover everything with a good grating of Parmesan. Cover with foil and bake for 20 minutes. Remove the foil and return to the oven for 20 to 25 minutes or until the top is all bubbling and golden. Serve immediately.

THE GREATEST CHORIZO BAKED RICE

- 220g chorizo, finely chopped into 0.5cm cubes
- 1 red onion, peeled and finely chopped
- 1 red pepper, finely chopped
- 1 tbsp olive oil
- 4 cloves of garlic, peeled and finely chopped
- 2 tsp smoked paprika, plus extra to serve
- 1 tsp ground cumin
- 50g Greek yoghurt – I use 10% fat
- 2 tbsp tomato puree
- 300g basmati rice
- 600ml hot chicken stock – from 1 stock cube
- 150g frozen peas
- a handful of finely chopped parsley leaves
- juice of ½ a lemon
- optional: aioli or garlic mayonnaise, to serve
- salt and pepper

Whether you're serving this baked rice as a showstopping side dish – it's magnificent with gorgeous grilled king prawns or a whole roasted fish – or simply piled high in a bowl with some shop-bought aioli, it is utterly divine. I use a little yoghurt to help keep the rice moist and then leave it to rest in the oven without any heat, so it cools gently, giving you perfectly fluffy, smoky rice, dotted with crispy nuggets of chorizo. Truth be told, if no one's watching, I can easily bash back most of this traybake myself, very happily.

SERVES 4

1
Preheat the oven to 220°C/200°C fan/gas 7. Chuck the chorizo, red onion and pepper into a 24x32cm roasting tin. Add the oil and plenty of salt and pepper. Mix well and roast for 20 to 25 minutes until everything is crispy.

2
Add the garlic, smoked paprika, cumin, yoghurt, tomato puree and rice to the roasting tin. Mix well so the rice gets coated in the oils. Pour in the stock and stir it all together. Cover with foil and roast for 20 to 25 minutes in the oven or until the rice has absorbed the liquid.

3
Scatter the frozen peas into the roasting tin. Cover again with the foil and pop back into the oven. Turn the heat off and leave for 10 minutes. I know this sounds like a mistake but what you want is for the rice to cook on a very low heat, so it can fluff up and the peas can heat through. The residual heat of the oven will do this beautifully.

4
Add the parsley and lemon juice and fork them through the rice, then scatter a pinch of smoked paprika over the top. Serve immediately, with aioli or garlic mayo if you fancy it.

PREP:
15 minutes

COOK:
1 hour

PRAWN AND FETA ORZO

I'm all about effortless cooking and this incredible Greek-style traybake is just bursting with flavour and takes minutes to prepare. The orzo cooks straight in your roasting tin with soft, squidgy cherry tomatoes, onions, garlic and a few spices. Chuck in a generous handful of prawns to cook at the end and finish the whole thing off with a joyous blanket of crumbled feta and chopped parsley. It brings those sunny al fresco vibes from the Mediterranean straight into the kitchen.

SERVES 4

500g cherry tomatoes
1 red onion, peeled and finely chopped
2 tbsp olive oil, plus extra for drizzling
750ml hot chicken stock – from 1 stock cube
4 tbsp tomato puree
400g orzo
2 cloves of garlic, peeled and crushed
1 tsp chilli flakes
½ tsp allspice
250g raw peeled king prawns
juice of ½ a lemon
a large handful of finely chopped parsley leaves
80g feta, crumbled
50ml just-boiled water
salt and pepper

1
Preheat the oven to 220°C/200°C fan/gas 7. Chuck the tomatoes, onion, olive oil and a load of salt and pepper into a 24x32cm roasting tin. Mix well and roast for 20 minutes in the oven until the tomatoes are lovely and squidgy.

2
Meanwhile, whisk together the stock and the tomato puree.

3
Remove the roasting tin from the oven and reduce the oven to 200°C/180°C fan/gas 6. Squish all the tomatoes into a pulp and then tip in the orzo, garlic, chilli flakes, allspice, stock and a pinch of salt and pepper. Stir together, then scrunch up some baking paper and spread it over the orzo and veg, making sure it's touching the stock to lock in the moisture. Cook for 10 minutes or until the orzo has just absorbed all the liquid and is al dente.

4
Remove the baking paper and add the prawns, lemon juice and most of the parsley and feta. Stir together and cover again with the baking paper. Return to the oven for 4 to 5 minutes or until the prawns are just cooked through.

5
Get your serving dish at the ready and splash 50ml of just-boiled water into the orzo. Stir together so it gets a little saucy and transfer to the dish. Drizzle over a load of olive oil and garnish with the remaining parsley and feta, then dive in.

PREP:
10 minutes

COOK:
35 minutes

CARAMELIZED ONION PASTA BAKE

500g onions, peeled and finely sliced
4 tbsp olive oil
1 tsp dried thyme
150ml white wine
1 bulb of garlic, left whole
160g cream cheese
400g pasta shells
120g Gruyère cheese (or vegetarian alternative), grated
salt and pepper

This is the perfect example of lux comfort food. Gorgeously creamy pasta, coated in a rich sauce made by roasting the onions with wine and garlic, then blending them with cream cheese until irresistibly smooth. Gruyère takes it to the next level, adding a subtle smokiness and melting into a golden gooey topping. It's sophisticated enough to wow at a dinner party – especially served alongside buttery roast chicken – but equally spot-on for a cosy night in on the couch.

SERVES 4

1
Preheat the oven to 200°C/180°C fan/gas 6. Chuck the onions into a 24x32cm roasting tin and add the oil, thyme and a good pinch of salt. Toss together and pour in the wine. Scrunch up some baking paper and wet it under the cold tap. Spread this over the onions, tucking in the sides, and roast for 30 minutes. Remove from the oven and give the onions a good mix. Add the garlic bulb, cover again with the baking paper and return to the oven for 30 minutes to caramelize.

2
Meanwhile, cook the pasta for 8 minutes until al dente. Scoop out some of the pasta water, then drain.

3
Transfer the onions to a food processor. Squeeze the garlic cloves from their skins and add to the onions with the cream cheese and 200ml of pasta water. Blitz until smooth. Check the seasoning, adding salt and pepper to taste.

4
Tip the pasta into the baking tray and pour over the sauce. Mix well. Add in a little more pasta water – start with 50ml and just keep adding little splashes until it feels really creamy. Top with the grated Gruyère and return to the oven for 10 to 12 minutes or until the cheese has melted. Serve immediately.

PREP:
12 minutes

COOK:
1 hour 20 minutes

GOOEY GOCHUJANG MAC CHEESE

500g pasta shells

1 x 400g tin of chopped tomatoes

250g cream cheese

2 tbsp gochujang paste – I use a mild one made by Sun Hee

a large handful of finely chopped chives

1 tsp garlic powder

900ml just-boiled water

30g Parmesan cheese (or vegetarian alternative), finely grated

150g mozzarella

salt and pepper

Sometimes in life you just need to treat yourself, and nothing hits the spot like a gooey, bubbling mac cheese. This oven-baked version is effortlessly easy, all cooked in one roasting tin. The pasta goes in uncooked with loads of cream cheese, tomatoes and – wait for it – Korean gochujang paste. This spicy, salty paste loves creamy sauces. It really mellows in them and gives them a bold savoury twist. Once the pasta is perfectly al dente and the sauce irresistibly thick, it's topped with a generous layer of grated Parmesan and mozzarella, then baked until gloriously golden all over.

SERVES 4

1
Preheat the oven to 200°C/180°C fan/gas 6. Chuck the pasta into a 24x32cm roasting tin and add the tinned tomatoes, cream cheese, gochujang, chives, garlic powder and a pinch of salt and pepper. Pour over the 900ml just-boiled water and stir everything together. Cover with foil and bake for 30 minutes until the pasta is al dente and has absorbed most of the liquid.

2
Take the pasta out of the oven and add the Parmesan. Mix well and check the seasoning, adding salt and pepper to taste. If you LOVE spice, you can also stir through more gochujang at this stage. Rip the mozzarella over the top and return to the oven for 15 to 20 minutes until all bubbling and a little golden. Let it rest for 5 minutes, then grab your spoons and dive on in.

PREP:
5 minutes

COOK:
50 minutes

THE ULTIMATE CAULIFLOWER CHEESE	200
PATATAS BRAVAS-ISH	202
CRISPY PARMESAN GNOCCHI BITES	204
LOADED SWEET POTATO NACHOS	206
CREAMY COURGETTE DIPPY SHIZZLE	208
ROASTED BEETROOT WITH HARISSA YOGHURT	210
SPICY CHIPOTLE GARLIC BUTTER MUSHROOMS	212
LUSCIOUS LEVANTINE AUBERGINE MEZE	214
RUBY RED CABBAGE SALAD	216
WARM BROCCOLI, BUTTER BEAN AND ANCHOVY SALAD	218
MEDITERRANEAN MELT - WHIPPED FETA AND PEPPER DIP	220
CHARRED CAULIFLOWER HUMMUS	222
BABA GHANOUSH BLAST	224

SIDES AND DIPS RECIPES

This chapter is a celebration of irresistible bites that are not quite full meals on their own – more picky bits, side salads and impressive dips that are perfect for sharing or adding a little something special to your spread. I love a table overflowing with food, and with these dishes you'll have everything you need to create that abundant look.

When it's done right, cauliflower cheese is one of the greatest dishes ever. To nail it, you have to use two roasting tins. Now, I know that's deeply annoying, but let me explain. You need a large tin to roast the cauliflower. It needs loads of space so it doesn't steam and gets a good char, which means you'll really taste that smoky cauliflower. Once roasted, you want a smaller tin to snugly submerge the cauliflower in the cheese sauce, giving that glorious contrast of a bubbling, golden top and a gooey, oozing centre.

THE ULTIMATE CAULIFLOWER CHEESE

SERVES 6 AS A SIDE

1kg cauliflower florets, cut into 3–5cm pieces
2 tbsp groundnut or neutral oil
800ml whole milk
80g butter
80g plain flour
150g mature Cheddar cheese, grated
80g pecorino (or vegetarian alternative), grated
¼ of a nutmeg, grated
salt and pepper

PREP:
20 minutes

COOK:
45 minutes

1
Preheat the oven to 220°C/200°C fan/gas 7. Chuck the cauliflower into a 30x40cm roasting tin and add the oil and a pinch of salt and pepper. Toss together and roast for 18 to 20 minutes until the cauliflower is just charred on the outside but still crunchy at the stems. Don't worry, we'll soften everything later. Transfer to a 24x32cm roasting tin so it's nice and snug.

2
Meanwhile, pour the milk into a saucepan and bring to a gentle simmer over a medium heat. The hot milk makes the white sauce come together much faster.

3
Melt the butter in a saucepan over a medium heat. Add the flour and stir together until claggy. Add a ladleful of the hot milk and whisk continuously until smooth. Repeat with the remaining milk until it's all incorporated and you have a lovely thick sauce. Reduce the heat to low and cook, stirring occasionally to remove any lumps, for 5 minutes. This will cook out the flavour of the flour.

4
Add 100g of the Cheddar, 50g of the pecorino, the nutmeg and a pinch of salt and pepper to the sauce. Mix well and cook, stirring occasionally, for 2 to 3 minutes or until the cheese has melted. Check the seasoning, adding salt to taste. Getting the salt right here will make it taste even cheesier.

5
Pour the sauce over the cauliflower and shake the roasting tin so the sauce settles in. Top with the remaining 50g of Cheddar and 30g of pecorino. Return to the oven for 20 to 25 minutes until golden and bubbly. Remove from the oven and leave for 5 minutes to cool down and firm up before serving.

PATATAS BRAVAS-ISH

800g of roasting potatoes, cut into 2cm cubes (leave the skins on) – I use King Edwards

2 tbsp groundnut or neutral oil

2 tsp Cajun seasoning

30g butter

4 tbsp tomato puree

1 tsp smoked paprika, plus extra to serve

1 tsp chilli flakes

100g Greek yoghurt – I use 10% fat

100g mayonnaise

1 clove of garlic, peeled and crushed

salt

This is my spin on the classic Spanish tapas dish patatas bravas, but with a cheeky twist. Golden, crispy cubes of potato are tossed in Cajun seasoning for an extra (admittedly inauthentic) kick, then served with two irresistible sauces. The first is a rich, buttery and spicy tomato sauce, while the second is a creamy, garlicky yoghurt mayo. The whole combo is finger-licking good – be warned, people will attack it like sharks! I love serving mine as a picky starter, but you could also have it with roasted chicken or grilled steak.

SERVES 4 AS A SIDE OR STARTER

1
Preheat the oven to 240°C/220°C fan/gas 9. Chuck the potatoes into a 30x40cm non-stick or lined roasting tin and add the oil, Cajun seasoning and plenty of salt. Toss together and roast for 40 to 45 minutes or until really crispy.

2
Meanwhile, melt the butter in a small frying pan over a medium heat and add the tomato puree, 4 tablespoons of water, smoked paprika, chilli flakes and good pinch of salt. Stir together so you have a lovely smooth sauce.

3
Finally, mix the yoghurt together with the mayonnaise, garlic and a pinch of salt. Swirl half on to a serving plate and top with the potatoes. Dollop over the remaining garlic mayo and the buttery tomato sauce. Do a final dusting of smoked paprika and dive in.

PREP:
15 minutes

COOK:
45 minutes

CRISPY PARMESAN GNOCCHI BITES

500g gnocchi

2 tbsp groundnut or neutral oil

15g Parmesan cheese (or vegetarian alternative), finely grated, plus extra to serve

2 tsp garlic powder

1 tsp oregano

½ tsp smoked paprika

100g soured cream

30g mayonnaise

1 clove of garlic, peeled and crushed

a handful of finely chopped chives

salt and pepper

If you ever needed proof of how much gnocchi adore the oven, this traybake is it. Roasted in a blazing-hot oven until irresistibly golden and crispy, the gnocchi are coated in Parmesan, oregano and garlic powder, then tossed in paprika for a smoky kick. Served with a luscious garlic and chive soured cream, they're like 'gnocchi crisps' – or 'chips' for my American friends. Now if this finger-licking treat wins you over (and it will), try swapping the seasoning for Parmesan and za'atar for an equally fabulous twist.

SERVES 4

1
Preheat the oven to 240ºC/220ºC fan/gas 9. Chuck the gnocchi into a non-stick or lined 30x40cm baking tray. Add the oil, Parmesan, garlic powder, oregano and a big pinch of salt and pepper. Toss together and roast for 10 minutes, then turn all the gnocchi over with a pair of tongs and return to the oven for 8 to 10 minutes or until golden and very crispy.

2
Add the smoked paprika to the cooked gnocchi and toss together – it would burn in the oven at this temp. Shake the gnocchi so they're not bunched up and leave to cool in the tray for 10 minutes. This gets them even crispier.

3
Meanwhile, mix the soured cream together with the mayonnaise, garlic, chives and a pinch of salt in a little serving bowl.

4
Place the bowl of soured cream on to a serving plate. Arrange the gnocchi around the bowl, and don't forget any crispy bits from the roasting tin. Grate over some Parmesan and serve immediately.

PREP:
5 minutes

COOK:
20 minutes

LOADED SWEET POTATO NACHOS

600g sweet potatoes, cut into 0.5cm rounds

2 tbsp olive oil

2 tsp garlic powder

2 tsp chipotle chilli flakes

½ a red onion, peeled and finely chopped

20g pickled jalapeños, finely chopped

juice of ½ a lemon

1 x 400g tin of black beans, drained

50g feta cheese

100g Cheddar cheese, grated

200g soured cream

a small handful of finely chopped coriander leaves

salt

Certain dishes go hand in hand with a delicious drink and these sweet potato nachos are no exception. They pair perfectly with an icy cold beer or, even better, a margarita. For me, it's a Tommy's margarita every time – just in case you're asking! The sweet potato slices crisp up beautifully, soaking in the flavours of garlic powder and smoky chipotle chilli flakes as they roast. They then act as a vehicle for multiple toppings: cheese, beans, pickles, soured cream and herbs. Before you head off to make them, I don't bother peeling my sweet potatoes. Life is too short. A good wash and a pat dry and they're ready to rock.

SERVES 4

1
Preheat the oven to 220°C/200°C fan/gas 7. Line a 30x40 roasting tin with baking paper. Pop the sweet potato slices into a mixing bowl and add the olive oil, garlic powder, chipotle chilli flakes and a good pinch of salt. Toss together and transfer to the roasting tin. Arrange into an even layer and roast for 35 to 40 minutes or until tender and crispy on the bottom.

2
Meanwhile, put the red onion and jalapeños into a small bowl. Add the lemon juice and a pinch of salt and mix together. Set to one side to let the onion pickle a little.

3
Remove the roasting tin from the oven and reduce the heat to 200°C/180°C fan/gas 6. Scatter the beans over the sweet potatoes and crumble the feta over the top. Add the Cheddar and return to the oven for 4 to 5 minutes or until the cheese has melted.

4
When the nachos are ready, slide the baking paper out of the roasting tin and on to a large chopping board to serve. Dollop over the soured cream and then scatter over the onion and jalapeño mix. Finally, scatter over the coriander and serve.

PREP:
12 minutes

COOK:
45 minutes

CREAMY COURGETTE DIPPY SHIZZLE

2 courgettes (about 500g in total)
2 tbsp olive oil, plus extra for drizzling
300g Greek yoghurt – I use 10% fat
a handful of finely chopped dill
1 spring onion, finely chopped
juice of ¼ of a lemon
salt and pepper

If, like me, you can't resist a table full of dippy shizzle to snaffle with drinks, this creamy courgette dip is a must-try. Grated courgettes are roasted until charred and meltingly soft, then combined with thick Greek yoghurt, spring onions and fragrant dill. The result is a luscious, slightly sweet and totally indulgent dip. Good things do come to those who wait, and if you can bear to let this sit for half an hour before diving in, the flavours will get even more irresistible.

SERVES 4

1
Preheat the oven to 200°C/180°C fan/gas 6. Using the coarse side of a cheese grater, grate the courgettes into a mixing bowl. Add the oil and a good pinch of salt and pepper. Toss together.

2
Transfer the courgettes to a non-stick or lined 30x40cm roasting tin. Spread them out evenly and roast in the oven for 20 minutes. Give the courgettes a good mix and return to the oven for 10 minutes until really wilted – almost looking like they have melted – and a little charred around the edges. Remove from the oven and leave to cool for 10 minutes.

3
Pop the courgettes into a serving bowl and add the yoghurt, most of the dill, spring onion, lemon juice and a pinch of salt. Stir together and garnish with the remaining dill and a drizzle of olive oil.

PREP:
5 minutes

COOK:
30 minutes

ROASTED BEETROOT
WITH HARISSA YOGHURT

600g beetroot
2 tbsp olive oil, plus extra for drizzling
juice of ½ a lemon
250g Greek yoghurt – I use 10% fat
3 tsp rose harissa
25g hazelnuts, roughly chopped
a small handful of roughly chopped parsley leaves
½ tsp Turkish pepper flakes
salt and pepper

This is one of my favourite ways to serve beetroot, roasted to perfection until super intense and nutty, then served on a swirl of creamy yoghurt spiked with rose harissa. The hot and cold combo is everything, and is borrowed straight from a classic Middle Eastern dish, *fattah*, a mouthwatering combination of yoghurt, vegetables or chickpeas, and crispy fried pitta chips. It's a textural delight.

SERVES 4 AS A SIDE

1
Preheat the oven to 200°C/180°C fan/gas 6. Give the beetroot a good wash. Then peel, trim and cut into quarters.

2
Chuck the beets into a 30x40cm roasting tin and add the olive oil and plenty of salt and pepper. Toss together and roast for 40 to 45 minutes or until tender. Add the lemon juice and a little more salt and toss together.

3
Swirl the yoghurt on to a serving plate and dollop over the rose harissa. You can swirl this into the yoghurt if you're feeling swanky. Top with the beetroot, hazelnuts, parsley and Turkish pepper flakes. Drizzle over a little more oil and serve immediately.

PREP:
8 minutes

COOK:
45 minutes

SPICY CHIPOTLE GARLIC BUTTER MUSHROOMS

600g chestnut mushrooms, stalks removed

1 tbsp olive oil

100g butter

2 cloves of garlic, peeled and crushed

1 tbsp chipotle chilli paste – I use Gran Luchito

a handful of finely chopped coriander leaves

bread, to serve

salt

There's something timeless about the classic combination of mushrooms, butter and garlic, a tantalizing trio that's always a crowd-pleaser. But throw in a dollop of smoky chipotle chilli paste and a side of fluffy bread to soak up those buttery, garlicky juices and you've got yourself one of the most satisfying starters imaginable. The secret to making the flavoured butter is starting with the butter at room temperature. But don't worry if you forget! Simply grate the butter with the coarse side of a cheese grater so it will mash together really easily with the other flavours.

SERVES 4 AS A SIDE OR STARTER

1
Preheat the oven to 220°C/200°C fan/gas 7. Put the mushrooms cup side up into a 24x32cm roasting tin. Drizzle over the oil and season with salt. Roast for 25 to 30 minutes until the mushrooms are tender and juicy.

2
Meanwhile, mix together the butter, garlic, chipotle chilli paste, coriander and a good pinch of salt.

3
Divide the butter between the mushrooms, placing it into the now juicy cups. Return to the oven for 5 minutes or until the butter has melted. Serve immediately with loads of bread to mop up all those beautiful buttery juices.

PREP:
5 minutes

COOK:
35 minutes

LUSCIOUS LEVANTINE AUBERGINE MEZE

2 aubergines, cut into 1–2cm pieces
1 red onion, peeled and finely chopped
6 cloves of garlic, peeled
200g cherry tomatoes, larger ones halved
4 tbsp olive oil, plus extra for drizzling
2 tbsp tomato puree
1 tbsp pomegranate molasses
2 tsp Turkish pepper flakes
juice of ¼ of a lemon
a small handful of roughly chopped coriander leaves
10g toasted pine nuts
salt and pepper

I'm a huge fan of aubergines – they're one of the most versatile vegetables out there and an absolute dream for soaking up bold, punchy flavours. Here I use them to make a smoky, tangy dip that's crying out for some crispy nachos or pitta breads to scoop it all up. The aubergines are roasted until irresistibly soft and squidgy, alongside plenty of garlic, tomatoes, a splash of pomegranate molasses and a pinch of smoky Turkish pepper flakes. Once roasted, they're mashed into a rich satisfying dip. The flavours develop as the whole thing cools, so it's a great recipe to make ahead of time for an effortless snack.

SERVES 4

1
Preheat the oven to 200°C/180°C fan/gas 6. Chuck the aubergines into a 24x32cm roasting tin with the onion, garlic cloves and cherry tomatoes.

2
Whisk together the olive oil, tomato puree, pomegranate molasses, Turkish pepper flakes, 6 tablespoons of water and loads of salt and pepper. Tip over the aubergines and mix everything together. Scrunch up some baking paper and spread it over the aubergines. Cover the whole tray with foil and roast in the oven for 50 to 60 minutes or until everything is super soft and squidgy.

3
Using a potato masher, mash the aubergine until you have a lovely thick dip. Add the lemon juice and mix well. Check the seasoning, adding salt to taste.

4
Transfer the dip to a serving dish and drizzle loads of olive oil over the top. Garnish with coriander and pine nuts and serve immediately.

PREP:
15 minutes

COOK:
1 hour

RUBY RED CABBAGE SALAD

800g red cabbage, cut into 2–3cm thick wedges
4 tbsp olive oil
juice of 1 lemon
2 tbsp pomegranate molasses
2 tsp caster sugar
70g feta cheese
40g pomegranate seeds
a small handful of ripped mint leaves
salt and pepper

Not only is this one of the most beautiful dishes ever, with the sultry red cabbage acting as the canvas for colourful pomegranate seeds and mint, it's utterly delicious as well. The cabbage chars up in the oven, intensifying the flavour, and then literally drinks up a sweet and tangy dressing that you drizzle over the top. It's incredible how a few ingredients can turn a fairly nondescript red cabbage into something irresistible.

SERVES 4 AS A SIDE

1
Preheat the oven to 220°C/200°C fan/gas 7. Pop the cabbage into a 30x40 cm non-stick or lined roasting tin. Drizzle over 2 tablespoons of the olive oil and rub all over the cabbage. Season with plenty of salt and pepper and roast for 25 to 30 minutes or until the cabbage is crispy at the edges and tender in the middle.

2
Meanwhile, whisk together the lemon juice, pomegranate molasses, caster sugar, the remaining 2 tablespoons of olive oil and a good pinch of salt and pepper.

3
Transfer the cabbage to a serving dish and drizzle over the dressing. Season with a little extra salt if it needs it (I find that anything charred generally does). Garnish with the crumbled feta, pomegranate seeds and mint. Serve immediately.

PREP:
5 minutes

COOK:
30 minutes

WARM BROCCOLI, BUTTER BEAN AND ANCHOVY SALAD

- 250g broccoli florets
- 1 x 400g tin of butter beans, drained and rinsed
- 4 anchovy fillets in oil, drained and roughly chopped
- 2 cloves of garlic, peeled and finely sliced
- zest and juice of ½ a lemon
- ½ a red chilli, finely sliced
- 2 tbsp olive oil
- 250ml hot chicken stock – from ½ a stock cube
- 2 tsp Dijon mustard
- Parmesan cheese, for shaving
- salt and pepper

Anchovies are such a versatile and underrated ingredient. For those who adore them, they're perfect straight from the tin, but even if you're not a big fan, they can transform a dish when used sparingly, adding a subtle umami depth like no other. In this recipe, they melt beautifully into a sauce of garlic, chillies and lemon, creating a vibrant dressing for charred broccoli and butter beans. I find that four fillets strike the right balance in this warm salad, but if you're unsure, start with one or two and adjust to taste.

SERVES 4 AS A SIDE

1
Preheat the oven to 220°C/200°C fan/gas 7. Pop the broccoli and butter beans into a 24x32cm roasting tin. Add the anchovies, garlic, lemon zest and juice, chilli, olive oil and plenty of salt and pepper and toss together.

2
Whisk the stock together with the Dijon mustard and pour into the tin to cover most of the beans. Put into the oven and roast for 20 to 25 minutes or until the broccoli is charred and tender, the beans soft and a little crispy and there's a little sauce left.

3
Transfer to a serving dish and spoon over all the lush juices. Shave over a load of Parmesan and serve immediately.

PREP:
5 minutes

COOK:
25 minutes

Ever since baked feta pasta stormed our social media, I've been hooked. I began experimenting with the concept, blending soft, baked feta with various roasted vegetables to create sauces, eventually moving on to this glorious dip. Here, the feta chars up in the oven, nestled between roasted red peppers, then gets blended with a dollop of yoghurt to produce an intensely creamy dip. The result is a perfect balance of smoky sweetness from the peppers and salty richness from the feta. It's an ideal snack to serve when you have guests over for drinks and dinner.

MEDITERRANEAN MELT-WHIPPED FETA AND PEPPER DIP

SERVES 4

- 3 red peppers, deseeded and cut into 3–5cm pieces
- 1 tbsp olive oil, plus extra for drizzling
- 200g block of feta
- 2 tbsp Greek yoghurt – I use 10% fat
- 1 tsp smoked paprika, plus extra to serve
- 1 clove of garlic, peeled
- juice of ¼ of a lemon
- salt and pepper

1
Preheat the oven to 200°C/180°C fan/gas 6. Pop the peppers into a 30x40cm roasting tin. Add the oil and a good pinch of salt and pepper. Toss together and roast for 30 to 35 minutes until soft and squishy.

2
Nestle the block of feta into the middle of the tin and drizzle over a little oil. Return to the oven for 10 to 15 minutes or until the feta is soft.

3
Transfer everything to a food processor and add the yoghurt, smoked paprika, garlic clove, lemon juice and a tiny pinch of salt. Blitz into a smooth sauce and transfer to a serving dish. Swirl it around the dish and drizzle over some oil. Garnish with a pinch of paprika, grab your pittas and dive in. I love to serve this warm – it tastes richer and has a smoother texture – but you can just as easily make it ahead and serve it at room temperature.

PREP:
5 minutes

COOK:
50 minutes

Anyone who has been following me for a while knows I'm fully obsessed with hummus. As Depeche Mode sang, I just can't get enough. It's creamy and comforting, garlicky and rich, and you can take it in so many different directions. Here I've blitzed roasted cauliflower into the hummus, which gives a wicked smokiness, and then added more as a garnish, alongside my go-to toppings of pine nuts, Turkish pepper flakes and a generous glug of olive oil. It's superb with pittas or crudités, or – my personal favourite dunking vehicle – Cool Original Doritos. Yum!

CHARRED CAULIFLOWER HUMMUS

SERVES 4–6

- 400g cauliflower florets, cut into 2–3cm pieces
- 2 tbsp olive oil, plus extra for drizzling
- ½ tsp baharat
- 1 x 400g tin of chickpeas
- 170ml tahini
- juice of ½ a lemon
- 2 cloves of garlic, peeled
- 10g toasted pine nuts
- Turkish pepper flakes or paprika, to serve
- salt

1
Preheat the oven to 200°C/180°C fan/gas 6. Chuck the cauliflower into a 24x32cm roasting tin and add the olive oil, baharat and a big pinch of salt. Mix well and roast for 20 to 25 minutes in the oven or until charred and tender.

2
Meanwhile, drain the chickpeas, reserving all the chickpea water from the tin (this super-starchy liquid will help the hummus go really creamy).

3
Transfer half the cauliflower to a food processor and add the chickpeas, 120ml of the chickpea water, the tahini, lemon juice, garlic cloves and a pinch of salt. Blitz until you have a really smooth and creamy hummus. Check the salt at this stage and add more to taste. Remember it will bring out the flavour of all the other ingredients, so get it perfect for you.

4
Swirl the hummus on to a large serving dish and top with the remaining cauliflower. Garnish with the pine nuts and a good pinch of Turkish pepper flakes or paprika. Finish off with a lush drizzle of olive oil. Grab your pittas and dive in.

PREP:
8 minutes

COOK:
25 minutes

BABA GHANOUSH BLAST

If I had to pick one dish that captures everything I love about Eastern Mediterranean food, it would be this vibrant chopped salad that's loosely based on the classic dish baba ghanoush. Soft roasted aubergines, peppers and tomatoes are tossed together with heaps of fragrant herbs, crunchy walnuts and a tangy pomegranate dressing. It's fresh, colourful and healthy without meaning to be. Perfect as a dip or a side salad, it pairs beautifully with everything but especially loves a charred smoky kebab.

SERVES 4

1 aubergine, cut in half lengthways

2 red peppers, deseeded and cut into 3 or 4 large pieces

6 tomatoes (about 450g in total)

2 tbsp olive oil, plus extra for drizzling

juice of ½ a lemon

1 tbsp pomegranate molasses

30g walnuts, finely chopped

a handful of finely chopped parsley leaves

optional: a pinch of Turkish pepper flakes

salt

1
Preheat the oven to 200°C/180°C fan/gas 6. Pop the aubergine, peppers and tomatoes into a 30x40cm roasting tin. Drizzle over the olive oil and add a pinch of salt. Rub the oil all over everything and roast for 50 to 60 minutes in the oven or until soft and squidgy.

2
Place a fine metal sieve over a bowl to drain the excess moisture from the vegetables. Start with the aubergines. Scrape out the flesh and finely chop it. You can discard the skins. Put the flesh into the sieve to drain a little. Next the peppers. Remove any obvious skin – you don't need to be too precise here – and finely slice the flesh. Add to the aubergines and toss with a spoon to get rid of any excess liquid. Transfer aubergine and peppers to a serving dish. Finally, the tomatoes. Cut them in half and finely chop, then put into the sieve and mix them with a spoon to get the excess moisture out. Add them to the serving dish.

3
Add the lemon juice, pomegranate molasses, walnuts, parsley and a good pinch of salt and pepper to the vegetables. Mix together and check the seasoning, adding salt to taste. Drizzle over a load of olive oil and garnish with some Turkish pepper flakes, if you fancy.

PREP:
20 minutes

COOK:
1 hour

INDEX

A

anchovy: warm broccoli, butter bean and anchovy salad	219
asparagus: summery orzo with creamy burrata	185
aubergine	
baba ghanoush blast	224
chicken and aubergine bulgur pilaf	67
Lebanese-Lancashire hot pot	154
luscious Levantine aubergine meze	215
Mediterranean roasted pork chops with za'atar croutons	118
spiced beef kofta and charred smoky veg	110
sticky gochujang aubergines	126
stuffed aubergines with jammy tomatoes	136
ultimate Turkish meatball traybake	125
avocado: roasted Cajun chicken with avocado soured cream	83

B

baba ghanoush blast	224
baharat-spiced chicken and sweet potato wedges	98
baked Italian risotto	186
bao buns: sticky mushroom bao buns	43
beef	
baked Italian risotto	186
coconut chilli beef rice	181
Croatian-style beef pašticada	153
harissa beef meatballs and giant couscous	26
Iraqi-style stuffed onions	163
Istanbul Express beef stew	44
Korean-style beef short ribs	145
meltingly tender beef brisket ragu	132
slow-cooked coconut beef curry	157
spiced beef kofta and charred smoky veg	110
ultimate Turkish meatball traybake	125
beetroot: roasted beetroot with harissa yoghurt	211

broccoli	
broccoli, goat's cheese and za'atar frittata	24
warm broccoli, butter bean and anchovy salad	219
browned butter dukkah pumpkin with herby hummus	109
butternut squash	
creamy gorgonzola and butternut squash stuffed pasta shells	189
hasselback squash with preserved lemon gremolata	114

C

cabbage	
ruby red cabbage salad	216
Vietnamese-style charred hispi cabbage	40
caramelized onion pasta bake	194
cauliflower	
charred cauliflower hummus	223
crispy cauliflower salad with jalapeño and soured cream dressing	31
ultimate cauliflower cheese	200
charred cauliflower hummus	223
cheese	
broccoli, goat's cheese and za'atar frittata	24
caramelized onion pasta bake	194
cheesy chicken melts	97
cosy gnocchi and bacon gratin	182
creamy chipotle chicken orzo	84
creamy gorgonzola and butternut squash stuffed pasta shells	189
crispy Parmesan gnocchi bites	204
gooey gochujang mac cheese	197
loaded sweet potato nachos	207
Mediterranean melt – whipped feta and pepper dip	220
prawn and feta orzo	193
ruby red cabbage salad	216
speedy prawn saganaki	32
spicy 'nduja cannelloni	178
ultimate cauliflower cheese	200
cheesy chicken melts	97

chicken
- baharat-spiced chicken and sweet potato wedges — 98
- cheesy chicken melts — 97
- chicken and aubergine bulgur pilaf — 67
- creamy chipotle chicken orzo — 84
- creamy Thai peanut chicken curry — 59
- crinkle-top chicken and bacon pie — 63
- dreamy creamy chicken pasta bake — 88
- Elektra's Greek chicken traybake — 64
- feta-licious chicken meatballs — 71
- Georgian-style chicken — 87
- greatest chicken shawarma salad — 60
- my quick-cook chicken adobo — 79
- Padrón pepper and chorizo chicken bake — 75
- Persian-style saffron chicken rice — 91
- roasted Cajun chicken with avocado soured cream — 83
- saffron and preserved lemon tagine traybake — 80
- Seoulful Korean garlic chicken — 72
- slow-cooked butter chicken — 68
- speedy chicken korma — 92
- sumac-spiced chicken with caramelized onions — 94
- tandoori roast chicken rice — 76

chicken adobo — 79
chicken and aubergine bulgur pilaf — 67
chickpeas
- charred cauliflower hummus — 223
- creamy tahini chickpea stew — 47
- crispy cauliflower salad with jalapeño and soured cream dressing — 31
- cumin-spiced lamb chops with roasted squash — 16
- Parma-wrapped cod with smoky chickpea stew — 28

chilli con carne — 150
chocolate: venison chilli con carne — 150

chorizo
- crispy gnocchi with burrata and green pesto — 166
- greatest chorizo baked rice — 190
- next-level chorizo shakshuka — 48
- Padrón pepper and chorizo chicken bake — 75

coconut chilli beef rice — 181
coconut, coriander and lime cod — 52
coconut milk
- coconut chilli beef rice — 181
- coconut, coriander and lime cod — 52
- creamy Thai peanut chicken curry — 59
- Keralan-style monkfish curry — 121
- Moroccan-style creamy coconut lentil soup — 51
- slow-cooked coconut beef curry — 157

cod
- coconut, coriander and lime cod — 52
- Mediterranean cod with herby Parmesan crumble — 129
- Parma-wrapped cod with smoky chickpea stew — 28

cosy gnocchi and bacon gratin — 182
courgette upside-down tart — 122
courgettes
- courgette upside-down tart — 122
- creamy courgette dippy shizzle — 208
- crispy seabass with zingy mint salsa — 117
- Mediterranean roasted pork chops with za'atar croutons — 118
- summery orzo with creamy burrata — 185

couscous
- harissa beef meatballs and giant couscous — 26
- Moroccan lamb with couscous — 149

cream
- broccoli, goat's cheese and za'atar frittata — 24
- cosy gnocchi and bacon gratin — 182
- creamy chipotle chicken orzo — 84
- creamy harissa sausage casserole — 23
- crinkle-top chicken and bacon pie — 63

pork tenderloin with creamy Diane sauce 105
quick-cook lamb ragu 170
sausage cassoulet with Parmesan crumble 135
slow-cooked butter chicken 68
speedy chicken korma 92

cream cheese
   caramelized onion pasta bake 194
   cheesy chicken melts 97
   dreamy creamy chicken pasta bake 88
   gooey gochujang mac cheese 197

creamy chipotle chicken orzo 84
creamy courgette dippy shizzle 208
creamy gorgonzola and butternut squash stuffed pasta shells 189
creamy harissa sausage casserole 23
creamy tahini chickpea stew 47
creamy Thai peanut chicken curry 59
crinkle-top chicken and bacon pie 63
crispy cauliflower salad with jalapeño and soured cream dressing 31
crispy firecracker tofu 39
crispy gnocchi with burrata and green pesto 166
crispy Parmesan gnocchi bites 204
crispy seabass with zingy mint salsa 117
Croatian-style beef pašticada 153
cumin-spiced lamb chops with roasted squash 16

curry
   creamy Thai peanut chicken curry 59
   Keralan-style monkfish curry 121
   slow-cooked butter chicken 68
   slow-cooked coconut beef curry 157

D

Detroit pizza 138
dreamy creamy chicken pasta bake 88

E

Elektra's Greek chicken traybake 64

F

feta cheese
   feta-licious chicken meatballs 71
   loaded sweet potato nachos 207
   Mediterranean melt – whipped feta and pepper dip 220
   prawn and feta orzo 193
   ruby red cabbage salad 216
   speedy prawn saganaki 32

feta-licious chicken meatballs 71

fish
   coconut, coriander and lime cod 52
   crispy seabass with zingy mint salsa 117
   harissa salmon with crispy lentils and garlicky yoghurt 36
   Keralan-style monkfish curry 121
   Mediterranean cod with herby Parmesan crumble 129
   Parma-wrapped cod with smoky chickpea stew 28
   quick-fire chimichurri salmon 20
   seared tuna with braised lentils and green olive salsa 106
   sweet chilli and turmeric roasted salmon 102

G

Georgian-style chicken 87

ginger
   Korean-style beef short ribs 145
   lamb biryani-ish with minty yoghurt drizzle 173
   Seoulful Korean garlic chicken 72
   speedy chicken korma 92
   sticky gochujang aubergines 126
   sticky soy and ginger pork belly 161
   sweet chilli and turmeric roasted salmon 102

gnocchi
   cosy gnocchi and bacon gratin 182
   crispy gnocchi with burrata and green pesto 166
   crispy Parmesan gnocchi bites 204

goat's cheese: broccoli, goat's cheese and za'atar frittata 24
gooey gochujang mac cheese 197
greatest chicken shawarma salad 60
greatest chorizo baked rice 190
Greek-ish lamb stifado 158
green olive salsa 106
Gruyère cheese 194

H

halloumi
- courgette upside-down tart — 122
- lamb cutlets with crispy potatoes and halloumi in a salsa verde — 113

harissa beef meatballs and giant couscous — 26
harissa salmon with crispy lentils and garlicky yoghurt — 36
hasselback squash with preserved lemon gremolata — 114
hummus — 109, 223

I

Iraqi-style stuffed onions — 163
Istanbul Express beef stew — 44

J

jalapeño
- crispy cauliflower salad with jalapeño and soured cream dressing — 31
- greatest chicken shawarma salad — 60
- loaded sweet potato nachos — 207
- slow-cooked pulled pork tacos — 146

K

Keralan-style monkfish curry — 121
Korean-style beef short ribs — 145

L

lamb
- cumin-spiced lamb chops with roasted squash — 16
- Greek-ish lamb stifado — 158
- lamb biryani-ish with minty yoghurt drizzle — 173
- lamb cutlets with crispy potatoes and halloumi in a salsa verde — 113
- lamb kofta with chips and dips — 35
- Lebanese-Lancashire hot pot — 154
- low and slow harissa lamb — 141
- Moroccan lamb with couscous — 149
- quick-cook lamb ragu — 170
- stuffed aubergines with jammy tomatoes — 136

lamb biryani-ish with minty yoghurt drizzle — 173
lamb cutlets with crispy potatoes and halloumi in a salsa verde — 113
lamb kofta with chips and dips — 35

lasagna sheets
- quick-cook lamb ragu — 170
- spicy 'nduja cannelloni — 178

Lebanese-Lancashire hot pot — 154
leeks: melted leeks with garlicky yoghurt and chilli butter — 55
lemon, saffron and preserved lemon tagine traybake — 80
lemon gremolata — 114

lentils
- harissa salmon with crispy lentils and garlicky yoghurt — 36
- Moroccan-style creamy coconut lentil soup — 51
- seared tuna with braised lentils and green olive salsa — 106

loaded sweet potato nachos — 207
low and slow harissa lamb — 141
luscious Levantine aubergine meze — 215

M

Mediterranean cod with herby Parmesan crumble — 129
Mediterranean melt – whipped feta and pepper dip — 220
Mediterranean roasted pork chops with za'atar croutons — 118
melted leeks with garlicky yoghurt and chilli butter — 55
meltingly tender beef brisket ragu — 132
monkfish: Keralan-style monkfish curry — 121
Moroccan lamb with couscous — 149
Moroccan-style creamy coconut lentil soup — 51

mozzarella
- creamy gorgonzola and butternut squash stuffed pasta shells — 189
- gooey gochujang mac cheese — 197
- speedy cheesy ravioli bake — 174

mushrooms
- pork tenderloin with creamy Diane sauce — 105
- roasted mushroom risotto — 169
- spicy chipotle garlic butter mushrooms — 212
- sticky mushroom bao buns — 43

my quick-cook chicken adobo — 79

N
nduja: spicy 'nduja cannelloni — 178
next-level chorizo shakshuka — 48

O
onions
    Iraqi-style stuffed onions — 163
    sumac-spiced chicken with caramelized onions — 94
orzo
    prawn and feta orzo — 193
    prawn and orzo fideuà — 177
    summery orzo with creamy burrata — 185

P
Padrón pepper and chorizo chicken bake — 75
Parma-wrapped cod with smoky chickpea stew — 28
Parmesan cheese
    crispy Parmesan gnocchi bites — 204
    Mediterranean cod with herby Parmesan crumble — 129
    sausage cassoulet with Parmesan crumble — 135
pasta
    caramelized onion pasta bake — 194
    creamy gorgonzola and butternut squash stuffed pasta shells — 189
    dreamy creamy chicken pasta bake — 88
    gooey gochujang mac cheese — 197
    quick-cook lamb ragu — 170
    speedy cheesy ravioli bake — 174
    spicy 'nduja cannelloni — 178
patatas bravas-ish — 203
peanuts
    creamy Thai peanut chicken curry — 59
    Korean-style beef short ribs — 145
    slow-cooked coconut beef curry — 157
    sticky mushroom bao buns — 43
    sweet chilli and turmeric roasted salmon — 102
    Vietnamese-style charred hispi cabbage — 40
Persian-style saffron chicken rice — 91
pizza: Detroit pizza — 138
pork
    Mediterranean roasted pork chops with za'atar croutons — 118
    pork tenderloin with creamy Diane sauce — 105
    slow-cooked pulled pork tacos — 146
    smoky pork meatball paprikash — 19
    sticky soy and ginger pork belly — 161
pork tenderloin with creamy Diane sauce — 105
potatoes
    Elektra's Greek chicken traybake — 64
    lamb cutlets with crispy potatoes and halloumi in a salsa verde — 113
    Lebanese-Lancashire hot pot — 154
    patatas bravas-ish — 203
    roasted Cajun chicken with avocado soured cream — 83
    Seoulful Korean garlic chicken — 72
prawn and feta orzo — 193
prawn and orzo fideuà — 177
prawns
    Keralan-style monkfish curry — 121
    prawn and feta orzo — 193
    prawn and orzo fideuà — 177
    speedy prawn saganaki — 32
pumpkin: browned butter dukkah pumpkin with herby hummus — 109

Q
quick-cook lamb ragu — 170
quick-fire chimichurri salmon — 20

R
ravioli: speedy cheesy ravioli bake — 174
rice
    baked Italian risotto — 186
    coconut chilli beef rice — 181
    greatest chorizo baked rice — 190
    lamb biryani-ish with minty yoghurt drizzle — 173
    Persian-style saffron chicken rice — 91
    roasted mushroom risotto — 169
risotto
    baked Italian risotto — 186
    roasted mushroom risotto — 169
roasted beetroot with harissa yoghurt — 211
roasted Cajun chicken with avocado soured cream — 83
roasted mushroom risotto — 169

roasting tins 12, 13
ruby red cabbage salad 216

S

saffron and preserved lemon tagine traybake 80
salads
    ruby red cabbage salad 216
    warm broccoli, butter bean and anchovy salad 219
salmon
    harissa salmon with crispy lentils and garlicky yoghurt 36
    quick-fire chimichurri salmon 20
    sweet chilli and turmeric roasted salmon 102
salsa 106, 113, 117
sauces
    Diane 105
    sweet chilli and turmeric roasted salmon 102
    sweet-sour 39
    tahini 114
sausage cassoulet with Parmesan crumble 135
sausages
    creamy harissa sausage casserole 23
    sausage cassoulet with Parmesan crumble 135
    spicy 'nduja cannelloni 178
seabass: crispy seabass with zingy mint salsa 117
seared tuna with braised lentils and green olive salsa 106
Seoulful Korean garlic chicken 72
slow-cooked butter chicken 68
slow-cooked coconut beef curry 157
slow-cooked pulled pork tacos 146
smoky 'nduja Boston beans 142
smoky pork meatball paprikash 19
soured cream
    crispy cauliflower salad with jalapeño and soured cream dressing 31
    crispy Parmesan gnocchi bites 204
    greatest chicken shawarma salad 60
    loaded sweet potato nachos 207
    roasted Cajun chicken with avocado soured cream 83
    venison chilli con carne 150
speedy cheesy ravioli bake 174
speedy chicken korma 92
speedy prawn saganaki 32
spiced beef kofta and charred smoky veg 110
spicy chipotle garlic butter mushrooms 212
spicy 'nduja cannelloni 178
squash: cumin-spiced lamb chops with roasted squash 16
sticky gochujang aubergines 126
sticky mushroom bao buns 43
sticky soy and ginger pork belly 161
stuffed aubergines with jammy tomatoes 136
sumac-spiced chicken with caramelized onions 94
summery orzo with creamy burrata 185
sweet chilli and turmeric roasted salmon 102
sweet potatoes
    baharat-spiced chicken and sweet potato wedges 98
    loaded sweet potato nachos 207

T

tandoori roast chicken rice 76
tofu: crispy firecracker tofu 39
tuna: seared tuna with braised lentils and green olive salsa 106

U

ultimate cauliflower cheese 200
ultimate Turkish meatball traybake 125

V

venison chilli con carne 150
Vietnamese-style charred hispi cabbage 40

W

walnuts
    baba ghanoush blast 224
    Georgian-style chicken 87
warm broccoli, butter bean and anchovy salad 219

Z

za'atar: broccoli, goat's cheese and za'atar frittata 24

THANKS

The biggest, boldest thanks, the warmest bear hugs, and the most thunderous high fives go out to every single one of you who follows me, likes, comments, and shares the recipe videos I create on social media. Without your incredible support, none of this would have been possible.

You guys have given me a new career, a fresh enthusiasm for food and permission to write a book like this. What a pinch-me moment, I can't believe it. Thank you all SO much.

I truly hope this cookbook slots into your busy kitchen schedules to become a well-loved companion. I can't wait to hear which dishes are your new favourites!

To make something quite so stunning takes a small army of brilliant people and it would be rude not to thank them all as well. To my agents, my publishers and the whole team dedicated to making every photo frankly lickable, cheers guys. We did it and I couldn't be prouder.

And finally, to my fiancé and family who are my biggest supporters, I love you guys. Oh, and don't worry, I will keep cooking Detroit pizzas on the reg.

Xxx John